The Spiritual Quest

Sacred Adventure Series

Book 1: THE SPIRITUAL QUEST

Book 2: MEETING THE MASTERS

Book 3: WORKING WITH THE MASTERS

SACRED ADVENTURE SERIES • 1

The Spiritual Quest

TEACHINGS OF THE ASCENDED MASTERS®
MARK L. PROPHET • ELIZABETH CLARE PROPHET

Staff of Summit University®

SUMMIT UNIVERSITY PRESS®

THE SPIRITUAL QUEST

For information, contact Summit University, 63 Summit Way, Gardiner, MT 59030 USA. Tel: 1-800-245-5445 or 406-848-9500.
www.SummitUniversity.org
www.SacredAdventureSeries.org

Library of Congress Control Number: 2003101393
ISBN: 978-1-60988-298-3
ISBN: 978-1-60988-302-7 (eBook)

This book is based on the teachings of the ascended masters delivered by Mark L. Prophet and Elizabeth Clare Prophet.

Summit University Press®

21 20 19 18 5 6 7 8

To those who see their whole life as a sacred adventure,
to those who push ever onward, daring to conquer,
daring to challenge the vast seas and to
scale the highest mountains of consciousness,
to those who remember always that
the trek upward is worth the inconvenience,
we dedicate this book as the next step on the spiritual path.

We offer this book with the greatest love to the ascended masters Jesus Christ, Kuthumi, El Morya, and Djwal Kul and to the messengers Mark L. Prophet and Elizabeth Clare Prophet, without whom it would never have come into existence.

SUMMIT UNIVERSITY®

A College of Religion, Science, and Culture

Summit University is a modern-day mystery school that teaches the science of the world's religions and the true spiritual foundation of all science. Students not only immerse themselves in a range of subjects in the fields of spirituality, religion, culture and science, but also experience self-transcendence through introspection, reflection, meditation and interactive learning.

In 1971, Mark L. Prophet founded Summit University in Santa Barbara, California, to provide in-depth courses of study on health, spirituality and consciousness. It was established as a college of religion, culture and science and served as a platform for the release of the original teachings of the ascended masters for nearly three decades. Ascended masters are the enlightened ones, the saints and adepts of East and West who have found liberation from the wheel of rebirth. While still in embodiment, they have influenced politics, religion, culture, literature and science in order to provide an ever-expanding platform for human evolution. Included in their ranks are the great spiritual lights of major world religions, such as Gautama Buddha, Jesus Christ, the Virgin Mary, Krishna, Zarathustra, Saint Francis and Bodhidharma. In the mystery school environment provided by Summit University, the ascended masters teach their students how to follow in their footsteps, make a difference in the world, and reunite with their divine source.

At Summit University, a variety of avenues for learning is available to the student, including home-study products, online courses and in-person seminars. Our online school offers extension courses at different levels, ranging from half-day courses to in-depth topical studies. We also offer a full spectrum of retreats and seminars in multiple languages at our campus in Gardiner, Montana, and select locations around the world. As our university expands, we continue to add new programs to our curriculum.

For more information about Summit University:
www.SummitUniversity.org
Learn more about our online courses here:
www.SummitUniversity.org/courses
Email us at: info@SummitUniversity.org

CONTENTS

ONLINE EXERCISES

This book contains a number of inspiring and transformative spiritual exercises such as meditations and spoken prayers. To do the exercises online with recorded audio tracks, look for this symbol to locate the links!

INTRODUCTION

Welcome! You are one of the people scattered around the planet interested in pursuing life as a sacred adventure—one of the relatively few who are willing to embark upon the upward journey of soul development and self-actualization.

The Sacred Adventure series is for those whose goal is self-mastery. It consists of several books that provide a road map for successfully traversing the spiritual journey of life while in the thick of everyday affairs. *The Spiritual Quest* is the first volume in this series. Its overarching vision of the essence of reality and being is not just theoretical, but practical. The book provides tools and techniques to help you meet daily challenges, fulfill your unique mission and reunite with Spirit.

The Spiritual Quest gives an overview of the purpose of life and presents a step-by-step guide to the spiritual path from the perspective of the ascended masters—our elder brothers and sisters of light. The ascended masters come from every era, culture and religion. They were once people living on earth just as we do. Through many lifetimes of devotion and spiritual striving they completed their earthly sojourn and ascended back to the spiritual realm from which they once came. Some of these masterful beings have chosen to stay connected with souls like us to guide us on the path of soul development and self-transcendence. Their teachings provide insightful answers to the basic questions of existence: Who am I? Where did I come from? Why am I here? What is the ultimate purpose of my life? Why am I in my current circumstances? Why am I with a certain group of people? Why do bad things happen to good people and vice versa? What happens after death? Did I exist before I was born? If so, where was I? Why is life a "sacred adventure" anyway?

Life is a sacred adventure because we are spiritual beings sojourning and living in a physical world, coping with the pull of the soul's yearning for reunion with Spirit while simultaneously living through the mundane experiences of corporeal existence. *The Spiritual Quest* explains how to engage fully in this challenge and reap maximum fruit from this experience. The topics are presented sequentially, building cumulative understanding and providing in-depth perceptions about life as a sacred quest. Readings, meditations and exercises for self-discovery are included as part of this practical pathway to help you discover new dimensions of yourself. By following the down-to-earth steps, you can enter a more rapidly ascending spiral of soul evolution. Invaluable tips and keys will help you achieve an amazing transformation of consciousness over the course of time.

Humanity evolves gradually and slowly, and most people are happy with this pace. They are largely concerned with meeting their basic needs, pursuing personal goals or seeking material comfort or wealth. While some of these things are obviously necessary, people with spiritual leanings recognize that there is more to life and they seek ways to feed their souls. The driving force behind this search is the spark of Spirit within them that spurs them on to higher understanding and can lift their souls to tremendous heights of spiritual self-realization. This summit of being is the goal of enlightened awareness, and it requires embarking upon an upward trek in consciousness.

The Sacred Adventure series presents a road map—including little-known shortcuts—for those who desire to accelerate their spiritual development. Following this path is not easy at times, but it is definitely a fast track to personal victory. Many have come to this point of understanding with a deep desire to change their lives, gain self-control and have more influence over their circumstances. Some have simply wanted more mastery over their emotions so that they are not so easily moved. Others would like joy, happiness, forgiveness and other positive states to spring more from their own conscious decisions than from the influence of others. Most have grown weary of material existence and find that the truths they have intuitively known are verified in these teachings. A few are seeking a self-study course in spiritual psychology. Still others have been led to these teachings because they want to know how they can make a difference in the world, how they can become behind-the-scene players who effect positive change on earth while carrying out their everyday affairs. A Sacred Adventure addresses all these desires and more. Whatever brought you to this path of yearning for Spirit, we welcome you.

The Sacred Adventure series is sponsored by The Summit Lighthouse, an organization that follows the wisdom tradition that began with the Theosophical Society in the nineteenth century and continued on into the twentieth century with the Agni Yoga Society, the I AM Activity and the Bridge to Freedom. In 1958, Mark L. Prophet founded The Summit Lighthouse under the direction of the Ascended Master El Morya. Both Mark and his wife, Elizabeth Clare Prophet, served as the messengers for the Great White Brotherhood[1] through this activity. Through these two messengers, the ascended masters released tremendous teachings that form the foundation for this course of study.

Each chapter in *The Spiritual Quest* begins with a segment entitled "Wisdom Teachings of the Masters," which conveys precious information that answers the vital questions of existence. In these sections, you will learn the mystery of your divine origin and your destiny as a masterful spiritual individual, transcending time and space. You will see what you

1. The word *white* refers not to race, but to the aura (halo) of white light surrounding the members of the Great White Brotherhood.

look like as a cosmic being and learn how to effectively plug into Spirit. You'll explore how to heal and purify your body, mind, emotions and soul and learn how to remain unaffected by negative influences. Discovering how to expand your spiritual centers, the chakras, will help increase your life force, and understanding how to strengthen your aura will empower you. You'll realize how your free will choices create karma—good and bad—and find out ways to balance the errors you've made along the way. And you will examine reincarnation as a unique part of the mystery of life. Finally, you'll take an insider's view of the ascension—the victory over mortal existence that is the ultimate goal of being.

Although the wisdom teachings of the masters do impart tremendous knowledge and convey great quotients of light to aspiring souls, in the end, the spiritual path is a do-it-yourself project. Knowing this, the ascended masters have provided an invaluable new technique for your personal journey—the science of the spoken Word. This one spiritual tool alone can accelerate your progress toward personal self-mastery beyond what you may have ever imagined. To that end, each chapter has a section specifically devoted to using and developing proficiency in this advanced system. The topics are arranged in an ascending spiral, with each succeeding topic being more advanced than the previous one, so it is best to read them sequentially. The online audio tracks accompanying this book can help jump-start you in using the science of the spoken Word on your own.

The Spiritual Quest provides a deep yet delightful understanding of the purpose of life that can instill in you a new sense of mission and destiny. The teachings of the ascended masters can literally change lives. May a Sacred Adventure be a joyous and insightful journey to the heights and depths of your soul and to the magnificent purpose that life has in store for you!

GETTING THE MOST OUT OF SACRED ADVENTURE

The Sacred Adventure series is an independent course of self-study that progressively leads you through the practical steps of spiritual development and helps you assimilate the teachings of the ascended masters. The following recommendations and study tips can assist you to maximize your enjoyment of a Sacred Adventure while reaping the greatest possible benefits from the material.

Recommendations

1. **Keep a journal.** This course is designed for use with a journal or notebook to record your personal insights and reflections. Journal pages are included for your use at the end of the book, or you may want to purchase your own notebook. You might want to reserve one section in your journal for your experiences with the exercises and meditations, and keep another section for taking notes.

2. **Begin at the beginning.** The chapters and books in the *Sacred Adventure* course are progressive, building upon the information previously given. You stand to gain the most by starting with chapter 1 in *The Spiritual Quest* and going through the book in sequence, and by regularly using the interactive components. You would then read *Sacred Adventure 2: Meeting the Masters* in the same way.

3. **Take a dynamic role.** Active participation will improve your ability to assimilate the wisdom teachings of the ascended masters. By practicing the exercises and meditations, you will also make the material more applicable to your daily life. It is recommended that you take advantage of the interactive applications (and the online tracks that guide you through several of them) by setting aside ample time and a hallowed space to practice them.

Study Tips

1. **Pick a regular time to study and try to stick to it.** Establishing a regular study rhythm and allowing time in between study periods can maximize your gains.

2. **Keep study periods short.** Research has proven that shorter study periods produce the most beneficial learning experiences.
3. **Frequently review the material.** If more than a few days go by between your studies, it is helpful to do a quick review of the information you last read. The review process reinforces key concepts and prepares you to grasp new ideas. If you have taken notes on the material, you may wish to study them before proceeding. Likewise, revisiting how you personally interpreted your experiences through the various exercises and meditations can help refresh your learning and bring new insights.

4. **Refer to the glossary.** The glossary included at the end of the book contains definitions and explanations for many terms that may be new or unfamiliar. Feel free to refer to it whenever a new term or concept seems unclear.

CHAPTER 1

Your Divine Origin

Cosmic Beginnings

What is the purpose of life? From time immemorial, people have asked this question. Attempts to answer it have filled volumes of philosophical and theological texts. The ascended masters have given us invaluable keys to understanding this cosmic mystery—keys that can open doors to fulfilling our soul's longing for oneness with Spirit.[1] This chapter presents the essence of these teachings on the purpose of the sacred adventure of life.

Understanding our divine origin can give us profound insight into our reason for being. This knowledge, placed within us when we were formed, can help us to unlock the secrets of our individual destiny. It also reveals our true nature as spiritual beings with tremendous light-energy at our disposal. We will begin by exploring how to tap into the powerful cosmic energy that was with us in the beginning—and is with us today.

Unraveling the Mystery of Creation

Who hasn't looked up into the sky on a clear night and wondered at the mysteries of the universe? It's easy to feel insignificant in the face of such immensity. Yet, on the contrary, the heavens hold the secret of the magnitude of our beings. The ascended masters have given us a beautiful vision of the connectedness of all life and the supreme importance of each individual to the divine whole.

Scientific inquiry alone will not uncover the master plan and our place in it. While modern science has begun to corroborate certain elements of ancient creation theories—like those of Hinduism and mystical Judaism—we can only begin to unravel the mystery of being by going to the place within us where God dwells. Here we can discover our unique mission that can help change the world for the better and accelerate our own soul evolution.

1. The use of *Spirit* or *God* does not exclude other expressions of the Divine. Likewise, because gender-neutral language can be cumbersome and at times confusing, we have often used *he* and *him* to refer to God or the individual. These terms are for readability only and are not intended to exclude women or the feminine aspect of the Godhead.

Both the blueprint for the mission and the light-energy we need to carry it out were placed within us when we were first created. So the first step to understanding this innate potential is to go back to the source, our divine parents.

Father-Mother God Gives Birth to Billions of Sons and Daughters!

In the center of the universe lies the hub of all physical-spiritual creation—the Great Central Sun, the principal source of the energy that sustains atoms, cells and man. Out from this spiritual sun have come solar systems, galaxies and billions of sons and daughters of God. In this book, "God" refers not to an anthropomorphic being but to the omnipresent Spirit of light, love and power that pervades the universe and is the source of all life. Spirit is the masculine polarity of the Godhead. In order for creation to occur, the feminine polarity must also be present. Therefore the Creator is, of necessity, both Father and Mother. And so our divine parents are referred to as the Father-Mother God.

In the Beginning, God sounded the Word that sparked creation. When he said, "Let there be light," and there was light, the Father-Mother God expanded the light by giving birth to individual Spirit-sparks. Each of these sparks was an exact replica of the energy of God's being. This energy is in perfect polarity—plus and minus, yin and yang, masculine and feminine, alpha and omega. This is how we were created in the beginning as pure energy in the image and likeness of God. By creating us, God could multiply his love and light.

Another name for the Spirit-spark is the I AM Presence. This is derived from the sacred name of God that was given to Moses out of the burning bush on Mount Sinai. When Moses asked God what his name was so that he could tell the people of Israel, God answered, "I AM THAT I AM." And so the Presence of God that was individualized for each of us is called the I AM Presence. It is the highest part of our being and is comprised of the same essence as the great I AM THAT I AM that is God. Our I AM Presence is an energy field of God consciousness that hovers above us and nourishes our bodies, minds and souls. It is fed by the light from the Great Central Sun.

"We are one" is a common phrase among brothers and sisters of light around the world. In reality, this is precisely the case. The I AM Presence of each one of us connects us to each other and to God. Although God has multiplied his Presence billions of times over, he is still one undivided whole. Since each of us bears an individual portion of God, so we are all united in that one Spirit. Thus, a web of light is woven between all people of light on earth. Truly, we are never really alone, but part of the one manifestation of the Divine.

The I AM Presence that was with us at our creation is still with us—even though it may not always feel like it. Our dense bodies are a far cry from the lightness of Spirit we experienced in the beginning. Because we have become so accustomed to material existence, we often forget that we are enormously powerful spiritual beings living in these physical bodies. What was once an effortless, natural state of being now takes work to even approximate. One way to experience this lightness of Spirit is to sound the Aum.

SOUND THE AUM AND RETURN TO THE HEART OF CREATION

One tool for accelerating our experience of oneness with Spirit is the chanting of the Aum (pronounced OM). The Aum is used for going into the fiery core of being. The Hindu Vedas describe the Aum as the one eternal syllable out of which everything that exists was created. Aum is the original sound of creation that has never ceased to sound throughout cosmos. The universal sound of the Aum accelerates our atoms and draws us back to the point of our creation in Spirit.

Intoning the Aum can help open our spiritual centers, or chakras, for the sound of creation to flow through us and raise us to planes of higher consciousness. The meditation below, "Experiencing Your Oneness with Spirit," includes the sounding of the Aum to facilitate going from an outer awareness of ourselves as physical beings to an inner awareness of ourselves as spiritual beings.

Meditation is one way of increasing our connection with Spirit and tapping into the light-energy-consciousness that is our birthright. Here's a meditation you can do to intensify your experience of communion with your I AM Presence and the Divine Presence of God in all creation.

MEDITATION: EXPERIENCING YOUR ONENESS WITH SPIRIT

This meditation is designed to help you experience oneness with the Spirit of your I AM Presence and the Great Central Sun—and to feel divine energy flowing through you. In a quiet place where you will not be disturbed, be seated in a meditation pose that is comfortable for you.

www.SummitLighthouse.org/SA1-1

1. Go within and focus your attention on your heart. You may wish to place your hand over your heart to help you focus your awareness there.

2. Breathe deeply several times until you feel calm and centered.

3. With your eyes closed, intone the *Aum* and experience your oneness with all creation. As you become more relaxed, begin to feel as if you are weightless, floating in space.

4. Visualize your I AM Presence as a sun of white fire, pulsating and radiating out rays of dazzling light.
5. Feel yourself merging with the brilliant light of this magnificent sun. Become part of the light-energy that interpenetrates cosmos.
6. Holding this visualization, give the first affirmation below three times to affirm your oneness with Spirit. Then sing the second affirmation six times to affirm your oneness with your Father-Mother God.

I AM Alpha and Omega in the white-fire core of being. (3 times)

I and my Father are one. I and my Mother are one. (6 times)

7. Intone the *Aum* to seal your meditation.
8. Return to the awareness of yourself as a person in a physical body.
9. Note the changes in your awareness in your journal.

Preparing for Mission Planet Earth

Far from being created as exact replicas of one another, each I AM Presence was endowed by the Creator with the potential to manifest individuality and creativity. Each of us was given a special mission as well as everything we would need to succeed in carrying it out.

Here's how we were individualized for this mission. While the essence of each I AM Presence is the same, God imprinted upon the fiery core of each one a unique divine blueprint. This spiritual blueprint can be compared to the pattern that was imprinted on the DNA of our cells when we were conceived by our earthly parents. Just as this earthly blueprint determined the color of our hair and eyes and whether we would be short or tall, so our spiritual blueprint holds the keys to fulfilling our unique destiny in life. It contains our divine plan—the purpose of being for which we were created.

This doesn't mean that our fates are predestined. God provided the matrix, the pattern. Once we descended into matter, it would be up to us to fill in the outline using our free will, which God also gave us so that we could be co-creators in the universe. The masterpieces we produce, the healing arts we practice or the causes of justice we espouse would be entirely up to our individual creativity.

> *What we are is God's gift to us. What we become is our gift to God.*
> —ANONYMOUS

This is one way that God continually transcends himself and expands his identity. The more we fulfill our inner potential through our own creations, the more the Spirit-matter cosmos expands. The Father-Mother God gives birth to Spirit-sparks and endows them with the seeds of light and energy that they will need in order to go out and express their individuality. Anyone who is a parent understands the responsibility and the risk inherent in such a venture. We bring children into this world and give them love and direction, but it is ultimately up to them what they make of themselves when they leave home and go out on their own.

Now, back to the Great Central Sun....

The Creation of Twin Flames

It really is true that we all have a match that was made in heaven! Our perpetual search for that perfect love here on earth stems from the experience of original wholeness and bliss that we knew with our twin flame in Spirit. In the beginning, we were created whole—alpha and omega, male and female. As an aid to understanding, the newly created Spirit-spark, or I AM Presence, can be visualized as a sphere of light, a whirling T'ai Chi containing the same masculine and feminine polarity as the Creator. The two halves of this whole are twin flames united in Spirit as one.

While still in Spirit, the I AM Presence of these twin flames traveled within the Great Central Sun, which is composed of spheres of light containing the infinite attributes of God's consciousness. As the I AM Presence journeyed through each of the spheres, it gathered around itself skeins of light resembling those of the Great Central Sun. According to the divine blueprint stamped on its fiery core, the Presence magnetized to itself the divine attributes and virtues that would serve as focuses for the soul's future initiations in the matter world. The light-energy of these attributes formed the colored rings of the causal body, depicted here.

After the causal body was formed, the twin flames separated into two identical spheres, as the alpha and omega polarities, for the purpose of moving into matter. Each consisted of an individualized I AM Presence surrounded by the causal body. Yet each half of the whole shared the identical divine blueprint that was impressed upon the white-fire core of the Spirit-spark when it was first created. In essence, this is how we were created in Spirit with our twin flames, our "other half."

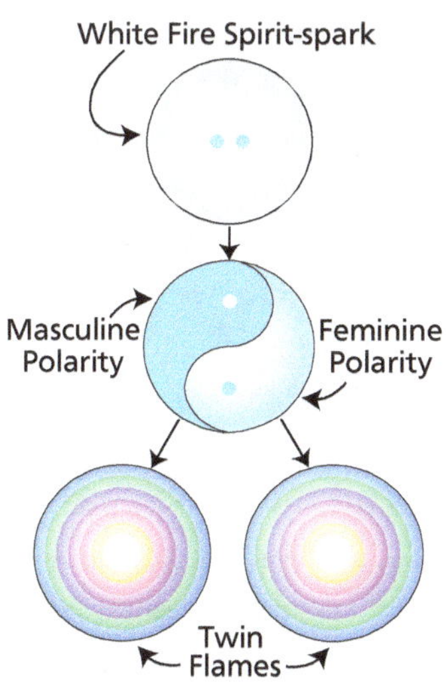

Causal Body

Because our twin flames shared an identical divine blueprint, they also shared a common mission. Even though they would later pursue divergent paths of creativity, the electronic pattern of their identity remained the same. The identity that we began to form with our twin flame as we cycled through the Great Central Sun formed the basis for the unique gifts that we now offer to the world. Thus began the journey of life with the beloved at our side.

From Spirit to Matter—the Soul's Journey

So how did we go from being Spirit-sparks floating in space with our twin flames to souls walking around on planet Earth looking for our "one and only"? When the creation of the causal body was completed, we moved out of the Great Central Sun. The I AM Presence of each twin flame projected a ray of itself into matter, and this was the beginning of what we know as the soul. In matter, one soul carries the masculine polarity and the other the feminine polarity of the whole. Yet the soul, whether it is housed in a male or female body, is itself feminine because it is the feminine counterpart in matter of the Spirit from which it came. Therefore the soul is often referred to as "she" or "her."

Twin Flames

Living in a new environment—matter—required adapting to completely new circumstances. Just as the I AM Presence gathered skeins of light to form the core identity of the soul, so the soul, after emerging from the fiery core of the Presence, gathered around herself skeins of matter to form the "vehicles" she would need to navigate in a new realm. These vehicles are the body, mind, memory and emotions.

Mastering the Energies of Time and Space

We went into matter with free will and the authority to "take dominion over the earth." "Earth" or "matter" is simply a densification, or mater-ialization, of the energies of Spirit in the dimension of time and space. Our reason for being in earth's schoolroom is first and foremost to develop, by our free-will consent, the masterful qualities that are a part of the character and being of God. Passing our tests in the schoolroom of earth would require gaining mastery in this new dimension as we worked on developing the inner divine blueprint given to us at birth.

When our souls first went forth from the Great Central Sun, we lived in a form of matter that was not the heavy, dense matter that we experience today. We lived in a dimension called the etheric plane, which is the highest vibrating plane in matter. We moved about in etheric light bodies in this heavenly world, guided by the masters and the light of our own God Presence. Our early life in matter was blissful. Many of us lived in mystery schools of the Great White Brotherhood and throughout the far reaches of the universe, where we walked and talked with the masters and lived in harmony with our twin flames and with each other.

Do you ever sense that life in this world feels "heavy"? Why is that? At some point in our evolution, we were tricked into ignoring the divine direction of our God Presence. It's the standard Garden of Eden allegory. By free will, we allowed ourselves to be tempted into thinking that there was a better way than the inner walk with God. We sometimes entered into compromising situations and made wrong choices. As a result, our vibration was lowered and our matter bodies became denser. In other words, we made negative karma, and we've been paying the price ever since.

Karma and dense bodies create the illusion that we are separate from God, but we are not. We are as much a part of Spirit now as we were in the beginning—and this journey through life is our opportunity to prove it.

Mission Possible!

Lifetime after lifetime we have desired to return to the state of love and wholeness that we knew in "Eden." Through many ups and downs along the way, we've done lots of great things and made tremendous spiritual progress. Though it takes some effort, paradise *can* be regained once we understand and apply the knowledge of communing with the I AM Presence. As the Ascended Master El Morya says, "The trek upward is worth the inconvenience!"[2]

As the Aquarian age dawns, there is a great spiritual awakening taking place on earth. It has been prophesied as an age of freedom, peace and enlightenment, a time of technological progress combined with spiritual development. It can be a time when the spirit of cooperation becomes the basis of every relationship—cooperation between God and humanity, and between people everywhere. This age gives us an ideal opportunity to accelerate spiritually and realize our divine missions so that we can unite as a powerful force for planetary healing and change. This is the time to tune in to our missions and go for it! However, this may sometimes be easier said than done.

When our souls first descended into matter, our missions were crystal clear. We knew exactly what we needed to do. Today that sense of mission may be vague or incomplete. And the experience of Spirit's constant presence may have diminished. Whether conscious of it or not, the soul retains the memory of its mission and its oneness with the Divine. She remembers a freedom of movement and consciousness not normally experienced in the physical world.

Our souls have been evolving as long as they have been sojourning in the material universe. When we first descended into matter, we were still very much aware of the Presence of God with us. As long as we maintained the connection

2. *Pearls of Wisdom,* vol. 25, no. 56, p. 505. *Pearls of Wisdom* are the published form of *dictations,* teachings of the ascended masters delivered through the messengers Mark and Elizabeth Prophet. Dictations are not the same as messages received by means of mediumship or channeling. When receiving a dictation, a messenger raises his or her consciousness to the level of the Higher Self. Simultaneously, the master lowers his or her vibration to that level, so there is a meeting and blending of the two consciousnesses. The master then directs the messenger's spoken delivery of the teachings.

with the I AM Presence, everything was fine. But after thousands of years of evolution, souls adapted more and more to the denser vibrations of matter. This resulted in a loss of memory of our origin, our home of light, and of the true nature of ourselves as spiritual beings. Perceptions became clouded, and many lost sight of their source and the mission they came to accomplish.

> *And so we went forth to be the manifestation of our Father-Mother God, sons and daughters who could put on more and more of those spheres of light which we call God consciousness. So it is in this God consciousness that we live and move and have our being. This we must not forget.... As surely as we are here and now, we are still in that [Great] Central Sun. We are in the beginning and we are in the ending. We do not have to get anywhere—we have to know who we are now. This absolute immaculate concept of our identity is the foundation of every quest and pursuit.*[3]
>
> —ELIZABETH CLARE PROPHET

Many experiences in the material world serve to reawaken within us the memory of the soul's calling. They remind us that there is a sacred purpose to life on earth and a divine mission to accomplish. Some already know their mission and are working to fulfill it. Others are still searching and seem to be waiting for the true mission to begin. Often a single lifetime will be devoted to fulfilling only a portion of the mission. For example, it may be someone's divine plan to be a great opera singer. But this may require taking preparatory steps, like spending a lifetime teaching children how to sing or learning to play the piano. In addition, we may need to spend time in activities and relationships that help us clear up our karma from the past while we're also striving to carry out our mission.

We are all emissaries of God. It is our reason for coming to earth. Each one has a special role to play in serving life, whether it's doing a particular job or imparting an essential virtue. We all hold points of light, points of identity as representatives of God. The key to discovering the meaning of life on earth and our special mission is to make contact with our highest spiritual self, the I AM Presence.

> *The soul is destined for such a great and noble good.... The soul must always hurry to this goal, that it can by every available means come to the eternal good that is God—for it is for that the soul was created.*[4]
>
> —MEISTER ECKHART
> (fourteenth-century mystic and theologian)

We are still connected to our I AM Presence, just as we were when we descended into matter. Answers to questions like "Who am I?" and "Why was I born?" can be found by meditating on the Presence. It can be helpful to repeat the meditation "Experiencing Your Oneness with Spirit" whenever you feel the need to renew the connection and receive direction from "above." Throughout these chapters, other valuable keys and techniques for drawing the light of the Presence into our lives will be discussed, including the science of

3. *Pearls of Wisdom,* vol. 29, no. 25, p. 228.
4. Meister Eckhart, quoted in Matthew Fox, comp., *Breakthrough: Meister Eckhart's Creation Spirituality in New Translation* (New York: Doubleday, 1980), p. 107.

the spoken Word. Over time, the I AM Presence can reveal to each one his personal mission—the most important contribution that he can make to life. With striving and a little help from our friends (on earth and in heaven), it is possible to be victorious and finally declare: "Mission accomplished!"

APPLICATION: STRIKING UP A FRIENDSHIP WITH YOUR I AM PRESENCE

The easiest way to begin communing with your I AM Presence is to start talking to this higher part of your consciousness, just as you would to your closest friend. When you need help with something, simply say, "Beloved I AM Presence, please help me to [insert your request here]."

This is a basic practice that you can remember when in a pinch. Developing a routine of calling to your I AM Presence for assistance could be the best habit you ever adopt. For example, you might be struggling to figure out the best way to solve a computer problem or to find something you've misplaced. The next time you encounter these or similar difficulties, follow this simple four-step procedure and see what happens:

1. Stop what you're doing and relax.
2. With reverence, ask your I AM Presence to help you.
3. Try again to figure out how to solve your problem or find what you were looking for.
4. Thank your I AM Presence for the assistance.

Initially, you may want to record the results of this experiment in your journal. You will be amazed at the high rate of success of this method in delivering instant illumination and direction in many situations. In certain circumstances, like trying to find a wedding band that you lost in the ocean, you may not get the results you desire. Sometimes the reason we don't get exactly what we pray for is that there is a lesson to be learned from a loss or difficulty that will help us grow—and ultimately our I AM Presence knows what's best for us. But you can be sure that every prayer is heard and acted upon, whether or not you see tangible evidence.

There is absolutely no limit to what you can know and do if you will but bend the knee before your own God Presence, I AM Presence. Know, then, that keeping the commandments and obeying the laws of God are prerequisites to your receiving the dispensations of God.

Yet, we shun no one. And we help, to the fullest extent of the laws of God, all who will simply look up to the sun of their I AM Presence and say, ***O God, help me!***

That is all you need to say. It is sufficient prayer. It allows the angels to enter your life and turn things around and set things right and direct you on your course to accomplish the mission that God has anointed you to in this hour.[5]

—ARCHANGEL RAPHAEL

5. *Pearls of Wisdom,* vol. 36, no. 15, pp. 202–3.

The Joy of Coming Home

The longing for the warmth and comfort of home is universal. "Home" takes on a new meaning when seen from the perspective of the soul's journey. The soul was not intended to remain on earth forever. We were given the opportunity to be here for a period of time in order to undergo certain initiations, gain mastery in the realms of time and space and express the love of the Creator as we carry out our individual missions. Having passed our tests in the schoolroom of earth, we could then ascend back to our home of origin for an entirely new adventure with our divine family in heavenly octaves.

Many of us have been here longer than we originally expected. As mentioned earlier, we got sidetracked along the way in different lifetimes. Yet we have had experiences that awakened within us the divine memory of our original spiritual estate and sparked a yearning to know our true identity and become who we really are. Our divine parents, the Father-Mother God, have never given up on us. They have patiently awaited our homecoming, inspiring us from the sidelines and providing angels and masters to assist us in answer to our prayers and hearts' longings.

Our return home is a return to living permanently in the consciousness of the I AM Presence. This is the ascension in the light that many who formerly lived among us have attained. Great beings like Jesus, Gautama Buddha, Kuan Yin, Lord Krishna and Mother Mary are just a few among these ascended masters. Others who never received outer recognition while in embodiment but who met the requirements to ascend are also among their ranks. The masters live in the etheric plane, which is the highest vibrating plane in the dimensions of matter. It is just as "real" as the physical plane we now inhabit but exists in a higher dimension.

I AM Presence

These brothers and sisters of light are joyously awaiting us. Until then, we can invoke these great beings into our lives here and now to help us on the path home. It's not necessary to wait until we get to heaven to meet them. They can help us to live a more heaven-filled life while we are still on earth. Future chapters will give deeper insight from the masters on the ascension process. They will also include more practical spiritual tools of spoken prayer and meditation that can help us develop an intimate relationship with the ascended masters that can further accelerate the soul's progress toward the ascension.

The Secret to Transforming Our Lives

The ascended masters teach that there is no greater power than the spoken Word to effect permanent change. Some contemporary students of the masters have used the spoken Word for more than thirty years to bring about profound change in their lives. Spiritual people from ancient traditions around the world have been using it for centuries.

Hindu, Buddhist and Jewish mystics believe that the Word is the source of all that exists. Indeed, several religious texts say that it created the world. If we believe the mystics, the Word is the most powerful generative force in the universe. If the Word can fashion worlds, just imagine what it can do for us!

Understanding the power of sound and its effects upon material and spiritual creation is good motivation to try it for yourself. For example, you can use the name of God "I AM" to effect positive change in your world, and this section includes some sample "I AM" affirmations. However, if the concept of the spoken Word is new to you or feels strange in the beginning, just remember the old adage "Nothing ventured, nothing gained."

The Word—the Power of Creation

Why is the Word so powerful? The Bible and the ancient Hindu Vedas say that the Word is God, or Brahman. In the Vedas we read, "In the beginning was Brahman with whom was the Word, and the Word is Brahman."[6] Likewise, the apostle John wrote, "In the beginning was the Word, and the Word was with God, and the Word was God."[7] And Genesis says that when God *spoke* the words "Let there be light,"[8] the process of creation began. The Word that was spoken was not just any word. It was the Word of God—a frequency released as the sacred word Aum at the origin of creation.

In the Eastern Indian view of the cosmos, the whole universe is an ocean of sound and light of varying degrees of density or luminosity. In this belief system, sound precedes light. This worldview may explain why God had to "speak" in order for the light to come into being.

---

6. Sir John Woodroffe, *The Garland of Letters: Studies in the Mantra-Sastra* (Pondicherry, India: Ganesh and Co., n.d.), p. 4.
7. John 1:1. All Bible verses are taken from the King James Version.
8. Genesis 1:3.

The mystics of East and West understood how to harness the power of the Word. They have connected with that force of creation by repeating spoken mantras and the names of God. The ascended masters have expanded upon this ancient practice by teaching their students a powerful form of spoken prayer called the science of the spoken Word. Today disciples use the Word in affirmations, prayers, mantras and decrees—a form of rhythmic spoken prayer—to draw the essence of divine light from the I AM Presence and cosmic beings into the planes of matter to bring transformation and constructive change.

> *You must recognize that you and God, as one, are the majority for the entire planet. You in God can change the earth! And when we multiply ourselves many times over through the science of the spoken Word . . . the union of our souls with our I AM Presence—and our oneness with the Great White Brotherhood through our I AM Presence—gives us a power untold. . . .*[9]
>
> —ELIZABETH CLARE PROPHET

Using the science of the spoken Word gives us a way to easily contact the ascended masters, the angels and our own Higher Self. Once we have made that contact, we can draw on the power of Spirit to bring about the opportunities needed to fulfill our life plans, to help others and to change the world.

Understanding that sound has the power to change matter helps explain why spoken prayer is much more effective than silent prayer.

Sound Affects Matter

Ancient Eastern sages taught that matter is actually the interplay of waves of sound. Hans Jenny, a Swiss doctor and scientist, demonstrated through practical experiments just how sound shapes matter. In these experiments, he used an oscillator to vibrate materials on various membranes and then photographed the results. Using a variety of frequencies, pitches and volumes, Jenny showed how sound can create intricate geometrical patterns and forms, many of which have an astonishing resemblance to patterns found in nature.

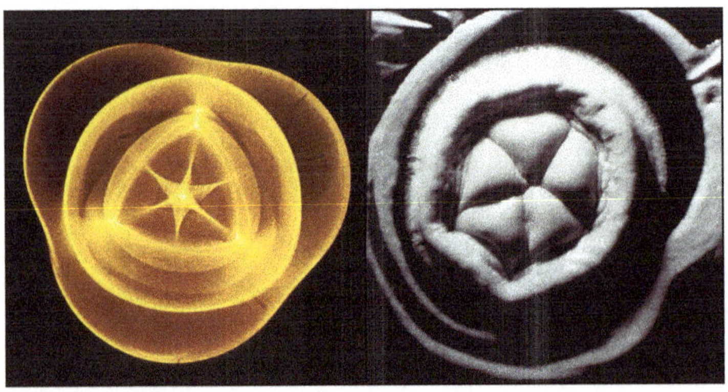

Images from *Cymatics, Vol. II,* by Hans Jenny; MACROmedia, P.O. Box 279, Epping, NH 03042.

Sound is actively used today to transform matter. Modern medical technology employs sound to clean wounds and pulverize kidney stones. Alternative medical practitioners use tonal frequencies to help heal

9. *Pearls of Wisdom*, vol. 38, no. 21, p. 220.

organs. Sound is even being investigated as an energy source to replace traditional methods of power generation. It is time that we begin to tap the creative power of sound in our personal lives!

Tapping Unlimited Power through Affirmations

Affirmations are the perfect place to start re-creating ourselves and the world around us by using sound and the science of the spoken Word. Affirmations have been used in schools of positive thought for many years to help people relax, to do better in a job or a sport, or to just become happier. They usually begin with the words "I AM," followed by a desirable quality or action. Some examples are: "I AM successful in my job!" "I AM a loving person!" "I AM overcoming all obstacles and limitations!" "I AM absorbing new material quickly and easily!"

The power in affirmations lies within the "I AM" phrase, which is derived from the name of God "I AM THAT I AM." The masters shorten this name to "I AM" when giving affirmations. In a spiritual sense, the words "I AM" mean "God in me is." So when we say the words "I AM" or "I AM THAT I AM," we tap into the unlimited light-energy of divinity and it is instantaneously transmitted to us. To experience this action for yourself, try the following short meditation.

MEDITATION ON THE "I AM THAT I AM"

1. Go within and draw your attention to your heart. Place your hand over your heart to help you focus your attention there.
2. Breathe deeply several times until you are calm and relaxed.
3. With your eyes closed, repeat the words "I AM THAT I AM" over and over again for about two minutes. You may also choose to visualize these words over your heart as you say them.
4. As you open your eyes, notice any changes in your perceptions. You may sense a greater attunement with your Higher Self or feel more centered within. You may even feel more energy in your body and aura, the energy field that surrounds you.
5. Perform this meditation as often as you like to increase the flow of light from your Higher Self into your world.

www.SummitLighthouse.org/SA1-2

Constructive "I AM" affirmations can be used to strengthen the qualities of God within ourselves. As noted in the Bible, Jesus Christ used affirmations with powerful positive associations such as:

- As long as I am in the world, I am the light of the world[10]
- I am the resurrection and the life. He that believeth in me, though he were dead, yet shall he live[11]
- I am the way, the truth and the life. No man cometh unto the Father, but by me[12]

Jesus understood that it was God in him, the I AM Presence, that was fulfilling the Word that he spoke, not his human self. In the same way, giving these or similar affirmations allows us to draw more of the eternal consciousness of the Divine into ourselves. Repeating affirmations and using them consistently over a period of time accelerates the process as our subconscious begins to assimilate the concepts. The positive thoughts then begin to work outward into our conscious awareness and we can see results. By using affirmations, we can re-create our lives and bring ourselves into much closer attunement with God's light and consciousness.

SPOKEN WORD PRACTICE: USING "I AM" AFFIRMATIONS

Try a simple experiment to see how "I AM" affirmations can work for you.

www.SummitLighthouse.org/SA1-3

1. Give the following affirmations with heartfelt intensity three times each. For best results, repeat them in the morning after you awaken and at night before you go to bed. You can also give these affirmations any time you need an infusion of light and energy from your mighty I AM Presence.
   - **I AM light!**
   - **I AM light/energy/consciousness!**
   - **I AM invincible and victorious!**
   - **I AM everywhere in the consciousness of God!**
   - **I AM the spirit of joy!**
   - **I AM love in action!**
2. In addition to these affirmations, you may wish to create your own to meet your specific needs.
3. Note in your journal any observations you may have as a result of giving the affirmations.

10. John 9:5.
11. John 11:25.
12. John 14:6.

CHAPTER 2

Your Higher Self

Contacting Your Inner Divinity

Reconciling the physical and spiritual aspects of being is probably one of the greatest challenges that spiritually minded people face. Those who sense the presence of Spirit within themselves also know that demonstrating their spirituality in the midst of earthly conditions is not always easy. Yet many have overcome the challenges of life on earth and achieved states of transcendent awareness. This chapter looks at some of the keys that ascended masters like Jesus Christ have provided to guide us in achieving these states of consciousness and attaining union with our Higher Self.

We can realize our divine wholeness more quickly once we clearly understand the components of our spiritual anatomy. Likewise, making the connection with our inner Source can be accelerated by learning about our Higher Self. Such knowledge can help us develop a more intimate relationship with these vital parts of our nature.

The Real Picture

It's easy to see the totality of our physical beings. All we need to do is look in the mirror. Seeing the full picture of our spiritual selves is another matter. Most people do not have highly developed spiritual vision that allows them to see what that Inner Self really looks like. So the ascended masters have given us a great tool to help us out. It's called the Chart of Your Divine Self.

The chart shows the relationship of the individual, as a soul in a physical body, to the Divine Self. And it provides a physical view of the nonphysical portion of our beings. It gives the total picture. The chart is a linear representation of what is actually a multidimensional manifestation of radiant, vibrating light-energy. In reality, the lower, middle and upper figures in the chart are overlapping fields of energy vibrating at different frequencies, from denser physical energy to light-energy vibrating at a higher rate.

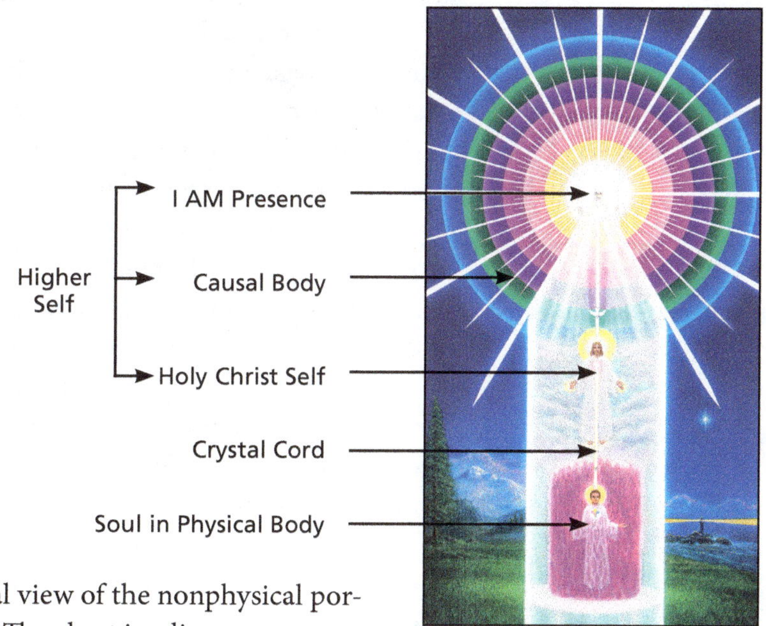

Chart of Your Divine Self

The Higher Self, depicted by the two upper figures in the chart, has been seen by people with highly developed spiritual sight. Some people who have had near-death experiences and then have later seen this chart have confirmed that this is the energy field that they saw around people when they were on the other side. Dannion Brinkley, author of the book *Saved by the Light,*[1] had three near-death experiences. He has told audiences that, in the unseen world, they look like the upper figures in this chart.

This visual tool can help explain the connection between the different components of our total being, which are both physical and spiritual. When it is clear how all the parts interact, it is much easier to create an intimate relationship with the Higher Self. And developing a closer relationship with this part of ourselves allows us to express more of the qualities of our divine nature in everyday interactions.

The I AM Presence is represented by the top figure in the chart. This is the Presence of God that is individualized in each of us. It is through the I AM Presence that we are united with God. The multicolored body of light surrounding the Presence is called the causal body. These rings of light look flat in this picture, but they are actually rotating spheres within spheres of radiant light-energy.

While the individual Spirit-spark was still developing within the spheres of consciousness of the Father-Mother God, the I AM Presence gathered around itself in space beautiful emanations of the divine attributes of Spirit that were intended to be expressed in matter. These skeins of light form the color spectrum bands of the causal body that reflect our true individuality. Each causal body is like a snowflake in its uniqueness. Saint Paul referred to the great individualized reality of each of our causal bodies when he said, "One star differeth from another star in glory."[2] Chapter 4 explains exactly what role this light-energy in our causal bodies plays in our day-to-day lives.

The soul is represented by the lower figure in the chart. How does the soul, which now resides in a dense physical body, connect with the vast storehouse of spiritual light in her causal body? The light descends to the soul through what is called the "crystal cord," or "silver cord," illustrated by the thin white line in the chart. Many clairvoyants throughout history have reported seeing this silvery cord with their inner sight. The cord, which originates in the Father-Mother God in the Great Central Sun, can be compared to the umbilical cord that ties a child to its mother. It is the lifeline that ties us to Spirit. Divine light-energy flows from our Father-Mother God over the crystal cord to the I AM Presence and then continues over the cord to the soul residing in the physical body. Before it reaches the soul, it passes through another part of our consciousness called the "Holy Christ Self," represented by the middle figure in the chart.

---

1. Dannion Brinkley with Paul Perry, *Saved by the Light* (New York: Random House, Inc., 1994).
2. I Corinthians 15:41.

The Holy Christ Self

It is known that all energy has a frequency, or a vibratory rate, and that Spirit has a higher vibration than matter. When souls left the plane of pure Spirit, they adapted more and more to the frequencies of matter and less and less to the frequencies of the I AM Presence. Once in the denser realms of matter, the soul required an intercessor to mediate the frequencies between Spirit and matter. The pure stream of light from the Presence no longer had a chalice in matter that could hold the light. So it became necessary to bridge the gap in frequency between the soul (which had descended in vibration) and the I AM Presence (which remained the pure essence of God). The mediator of this light is a level of consciousness called the "Holy Christ Self." It is variously referred to by the ascended masters and other spiritual sources as the "Higher Mental Body," the "Christ consciousness" or the "Krishna consciousness."

Here's why a mediator is needed: If the intense light of the I AM Presence were to suddenly descend into the physical body, the body would not be able to contain it. This can be compared to plugging a 12-volt appliance into a 120-volt outlet. The current from the outlet would blow out the appliance. However, if the appliance had an adapter attached to it, the current would be stepped down so that it could operate the appliance without destroying it. Similarly, in order for us to use the powerful light-energy of the I AM Presence, it needs to be stepped down to a level that can be handled without "blowing" our circuits. So the Holy Christ Self serves as the adapter or step-down transformer.

Holy Christ Self

Two thousand years ago, Jesus Christ fulfilled the role of mediator between God and the people. He was able to do this because he had attained the consciousness of the Holy Christ Self. This is why he was called "the Christ." The word *Christ* is derived from the Greek word *christos,* meaning "anointed." One who is Christ is anointed with the light of the Father-Mother God, or the I AM Presence. The light of Spirit flows freely through such a person, who then uses it to bless and heal other parts of life.

In his ministry, Jesus conveyed to the people the love and wisdom of the Father in order to show them the way back to God. The Holy Christ Self is a level of consciousness that can bring us closer to the Divine. When Jesus said to his disciples, "I am the way, the truth and the life. No man cometh unto the Father, but by me,"[3] he was saying that in order to reach the Father (who is one with the Mother), we need to get there by way of the Christ consciousness.

By examining the qualities that Jesus displayed through his words and actions, one comes to understand what it means to embody the Christ consciousness.

3. John 14:6.

Jesus

Jesus set an example that each person desiring divine union can follow. When he said, "He that believeth on me [the Christ], the works that I do shall he do also,"[4] Jesus was saying that everyone has the potential to achieve what he did. This does not mean that it is necessary to perform miracles. It means that by embodying the qualities that Jesus demonstrated, like forgiveness, compassion, love, peace, truth, surrender, humility, strength and obedience to spiritual laws, others can attain the same Christ consciousness that Jesus achieved.

One way to move toward this goal of Christ consciousness is to make a habit of evaluating one's own character traits. The devotee who wishes to assess her strengths and weaknesses can ask, "How do I manifest these good or bad qualities in large and small ways?" Or, when faced with difficult situations, she might say, "What would Jesus do?" In Hinduism, Krishna represents the Christ consciousness. So those who feel more of an affinity with the Eastern tradition might ask, "What would Krishna do?" The Christ consciousness will increase day by day, little by little as the devotee seeks to emulate the virtues that Christ personified.

Krishna

The Christ Self acts as our discriminating intelligence. In the human condition, it is hard to always know what is in our own best interests. It's easy to be swayed by desires or habits that may not be beneficial to our spiritual development. Our Christ Self always knows what is best for us in every situation. It knows what is required at every moment. When our soul is attuned to the vibration of the Christ Self, she can draw forth from the I AM Presence the precise amount of light, energy and illumination needed to accomplish her goals.

The assistance of the Presence can be invoked through the spoken Word in the name and by the authority of the Christ Self. This is because the Christ Self has the power to determine and dispense the light-energy that is in keeping with God's will. In the "Liberating Power of the Word" section in chapter 3, you will have the opportunity to call forth spiritual light by the authority of your Christ Self using the science of the spoken Word.

The Christ Self translates the vibrations, the love and the messages of the I AM Presence. This communication comes as the voice of conscience, which is the voice of the Christ Self. Listening to the

4. John 14:12.

Holy Christ Self provides unerring direction. Mahatma Gandhi once said, "The only tyrant I accept in this world is the 'still small voice' within."[7] He was saying that this voice was the only authority he would obey without question. He perceived that inner voice as his means of staying on course and fulfilling his goals.

Gandhi

Most everyone has heard the voice of conscience telling them to do or not do something. And we've probably all experienced the consequences of not listening to that still, small voice speaking to us. How many times have we said to ourselves, "Why didn't I listen?"

Learning to recognize the voice of the Christ Self helps develop a greater sensitivity to this aspect of consciousness. As we integrate more fully with this part of ourselves, we gain greater grace and mastery in handling life's daily challenges. We come more into harmony with the flow of life.

Your Holy Christ Self, in its wisdom, sees all your requirements and is aware of each lesson your lifestream needs in order to fulfill its own life plan and will give you daily the guiding ray of Christ intelligence which is constantly pouring forth from the Holy Christ Self above you—which is your mediator. . . .

You see, the Presence of God is of too pure eyes to behold iniquity[5] *(inequity or unbalance) but all phases of earthly and heavenly states of consciousness can be equally perceived and understood by your own Holy Christ Self in its role of "mediator" between God and man! For this Christ Self descended from the Presence itself to act as God your Saviour—and is the only true mediator between God (the Presence of God I AM in you) and your own unascended individualized self. Revere then the service this Christ Self renders you, my dear ones, for it is indeed unique!*[6]

—THE ASCENDED MASTER THE MAHA CHOHAN

---

5. Habakkuk 1:13.
6. *Pearls of Wisdom,* vol. 3, no. 4, p. 2.
7. Mohandas K. Gandhi, quoted in Richard Attenborough, comp., *The Words of Gandhi* (New York: Newmarket Press, 1982), p. 20.

I never know when my Higher Self is going to step in and make a difference in my life. For example, one fine spring day when I was at Boston University, I was hurrying out the door of my dorm when I heard an inner voice say, "Put on your heavy winter coat." I knew which coat. It was thick and lined with fake alpaca fur. I thought to myself, "OK, this is the craziest thing I've ever heard of, but I'll put it on."

But my Higher Self wasn't satisfied. "Put on your heavy gloves," said the voice. "This is not for real," I said to myself. "I'll put on the coat, but I am not going to put on these heavy gloves. It's just too hot!"

So I put on the coat and ran down the street, nearly late for my class. I crossed a street between some cars that were stopped at a light—and bam! A bicycle came speeding alongside one of the cars and ran right into me. It knocked me to the ground and I caught myself on my unprotected hands. I landed in a jumble, with my body insulated by the coat but my hands scraped up.

My Higher Self had saved me from serious injury, but it couldn't save me from my own stubbornness. The lesson I learned that day is that being in touch with my Higher Self is more valuable than anything else in my life.[8]

—ELIZABETH CLARE PROPHET

APPLICATION: SHARPENING YOUR INNER LISTENING SKILLS

This two-part exercise will give you an opportunity to reflect upon situations in your life when your Christ Self was talking to you. It can help you to recognize your inner voice, to observe your reactions upon hearing it, and to alert you to the consequences of heeding or not heeding it.

Part 1: Why Didn't I Listen?

1. Think back to a time when you were prompted by your inner voice to do something and you didn't listen. This could be a minor incident like receiving a prompting to take your umbrella to work with you in the morning even though the sun was shining, and then it rained later in the day. Or it might be a situation that had more far-reaching consequences.

2. Note in your journal the answers to the following questions:
   - What did the voice say?
   - What did the voice "sound" like? Was it soft, loud, harsh, loving?
   - Why didn't I listen?
   - What happened as a result of my not listening, if anything?

3. If you remember the thought process you went through between the time that you heard the voice and the time you made the decision not to follow its direction, write this down in your journal.

8. Elizabeth Clare Prophet, *Access the Power of Your Higher Self* (Gardiner, Mont.: Summit University Press, 1997), pp. 1–2.

Part 2: What Happened When I Did Listen?

1. Now think back on a time when you were prompted by your inner voice to do something and you *did* listen.
2. Try to remember what prompted you to listen and record your recollections in your journal.
3. What were the consequences of following the direction of your inner voice? Write these in your journal.

> *Above all, do not let a day go by that you do not commune with your Holy Christ Self. For your Holy Christ Self is your immortal Self. And if you are to attain union with God, it is with this Self that you must become one. Therefore, strive you must to maintain unbroken communion with your Holy Christ Self. This communion can be perpetual, waking or sleeping.*[9]
>
> —THE ASCENDED MASTER JESUS CHRIST

It is often difficult to hear the quiet voice of the Holy Christ Self speaking over all the noise and distraction of the outer world and the physical senses. So how can we best develop a listening ear to receive its direction? The mystics and saints of all ages have given us the key. The place to go to commune with the Divine is in the heart.

The Heart Center—Doorway to the Divine

The heart is the soul's link to divinity. This is because the I AM Presence placed a spiritual flame—the essence of itself—in each one's heart center. This flame is also the essence of God, because the I AM Presence is an emanation of God. This flame in the interior of our being connects us with our divine point of origin in the Great Central Sun.

The flame is located in a spiritual center called the "secret chamber of the heart." In the Hindu tradition, the Katha Upanishad speaks of the "light of the Spirit" that is concealed in the "secret high place of the heart" of all beings. This is the place we go to intensify the experience of Spirit. It is the space we enter to commune with the Holy Christ Self and receive the light of the I AM Presence. Some people experience a burning sensation in the area of the heart when they feel intense love for others or for God. This is testimony to the presence of the flame residing deep within.

> *The light that shines beyond all things on earth, beyond us all . . . this is the light that shines in our hearts.*[10]
>
> —CHANDOGYA UPANISHAD (sacred Hindu text)

9. *Pearls of Wisdom,* vol. 39, no. 31, p. 172.
10. Chandogya Upanishad 3.13, 14, quoted in Kathleen Healy, *Entering the Cave of the Heart: Eastern Ways of Prayer for Western Christians* (New York: Paulist Press, 1986), p. 102.

People too often seek God outside of themselves. It is true that God is everywhere. Yet it is not necessary to go further than the heart's secret chamber to connect with that power. Divinely inspired solutions to all problems can be found in this interior focus. Jesus said, "The kingdom of God is within you,"[11] meaning that the heart center is the place to contact Spirit and realize divine consciousness. Other religions teach the same principle. Buddhists speak of the "germ of Buddhahood," or Buddha nature, that exists in every living being. The Sanskrit word *Atman* is used in the Upanishads to mean the indwelling God—the imperishable, undecaying core of man. Atman is identical with Brahman, who is the eternal, absolute being, absolute consciousness and absolute bliss.

After an arduous journey across the Himalayas, a young seeker arrived at the cave of an old hermit.

"Where are you going?" the hermit asked.

"To find Shambhala," the youth replied.

"Ah! Well, then, you need not travel far," the hermit said. "For the kingdom of Shambhala is in your heart."[12]

—TIBETAN LEGEND

The fourteenth century Christian theologian and mystic Meister Eckhart taught of the flame within the heart's secret chamber when he said, "God's seed is within us."[13] He said there is a part of us that "remains eternally in the Spirit and is divine.... Here God glows and flames without ceasing."[14] The ascended masters call this flame the "divine spark" or the "threefold flame." They also call it the "Holy Christ flame" because through this flame we commune with the Christ Self.

The Ascended Master Zarathustra talked about how the sacred spark within is the nucleus of the all-encompassing Spirit: "Because you have that something, you can become that all-in-all. You can enter the heart of the flame in the acorn of self and know that because God is there and is that fire, you will be all that you are and that in fact, in embryo, in potential, you are already that God, one in the universal mind."[15]

11. Luke 17:21.
12. Adapted from legend told by Edwin Bernbaum in "The Hidden Kingdom of Shambhala," *Natural History* 92, no. 4 (April 1983): 55–56, 59, 62.
13. M. O'C. Walshe, trans. and ed., *Meister Eckhart: Sermons and Treatises* (Longmead, Shaftesbury, Dorset: Element Books, 1987), 3:107.
14. Meister Eckhart, quoted in Joseph James, comp., *The Way of Mysticism* (New York: Harper and Brothers Publishers, n.d.), p. 64.
15. *Pearls of Wisdom*, vol. 29, no. 41, p. 382.

Divine Power, Wisdom and Love: Use It or Lose It

The flame in the secret chamber of the heart is called "threefold" because it has three fiery plumes. Each plume represents one aspect of the divine Trinity —Father, Son and Holy Spirit or, in Hindu terminology, Brahma, Vishnu and Shiva. The flame in the heart is also called threefold because it embodies the three primary attributes of Spirit: power, wisdom and love. The elements of the Trinity, as well as their corresponding qualities, are represented by the colors blue (Father/power), yellow (Son/wisdom) and pink (Holy Spirit/love). The fiery core from which the threefold flame springs corresponds to the Mother/matter aspect of God and is represented by the color white.

DIVINE QUALITIES OF THE THREEFOLD FLAME		
Father	Son	Holy Spirit
Power	Wisdom	Love
Blue	Yellow	Pink

Threefold Flame

So what does the triune nature of this spiritual flame mean to the individual? By exercising the divine qualities of the threefold flame, one can manifest the trinity of God's consciousness and experience greater mastery in whatever he does. Here's why. The pink plume is the fire of creativity born of the love, compassion and grace of the Holy Spirit that can help endow all creation with that Spirit. The golden yellow plume represents the Son of wisdom, the mind of Christ within that bestows discriminating intelligence. And the blue plume contains the power and determination of the Father that can bring into manifestation the soul's divine blueprint.

These godly qualities exist as a wonderful potential within the heart. They need to be applied and developed in order to become a reality in daily life. The flame can be compared to a seed, whose potential is locked inside it. The seed requires tending and nurturing or it will remain dormant. Offering loving devotion to this threefold flame in meditation and spoken prayer helps it to grow. Kind thoughts, words and actions increase and intensify it. They create a powerful magnet for more of the light of the Christ Self to fill the heart center. These actions as practiced by Jesus and many other masters helped them to attain their Christhood and achieve their final immortality in the ritual of the ascension, discussed in chapter 7.

The threefold flame is the soul's passport to immortality. It is the part of one's material existence that is pure Spirit, and only that which is Spirit can endure forever. The soul, on the other hand, is mortal. It is a nonpermanent aspect of being. Because the soul has free will, it can choose at any time to stop pursuing its divinity. It can choose to ignore the promptings of the Holy Christ Self to rise in consciousness. Or it can choose to follow a path of devotion through the threefold flame that leads to oneness with the Christ Self. The soul must be fully bonded to the Christ Self before it can unite with the I AM Presence in the ascension and become immortal. This bonding is a process that can happen day by day. It is a process whereby the soul makes choices and learns lessons that lead to self-mastery and the awareness of self as Spirit.

> *In the flame you know that you have always existed and that you always will. In the flame is the merging of your soul and your Spirit in eternity.*[16]
>
> —THE ASCENDED MASTER EL MORYA

Meditating on the Flame

The stresses of life are accelerating with the fast pace of the twenty-first century. Human solutions to the increasingly complex problems of our time no longer suffice. Divine solutions are the need of the hour. It is more important than ever to enter into the stillness of the heart's interior—to that place of peace and centeredness of inner divinity—to shed light upon every challenge we face both personally and collectively. By developing a daily habit of going into the heart to simply talk and pray to the Holy Christ Self, we can increase our receptivity to the direction of the inner voice. Meditating on the threefold flame is a practice that can lead the soul from a condition of outer awareness to a profound inner connection with divine Reality. The flame can then act as a catalyst, a "spark plug," to activate a close attunement with the I AM Presence.

It is helpful to meditate on the flame in the secret chamber of the heart.

Secret Chamber of the Heart

The secret chamber can be thought of as a private meditation room, an interior castle, as Saint Teresa of Avila called it. In the Hindu tradition, the devotee visualizes a jeweled island in his heart. There he sees himself before a beautiful altar, where he worships his teacher in deep meditation.

Jesus spoke of entering the secret chamber of the heart when he said, "When thou prayest, enter into thy closet. And when thou hast shut thy door, pray to thy Father which is in secret; and thy Father which seeth in secret shall reward thee openly."[17] This closet that Jesus spoke of symbolizes going into another dimension of consciousness. It is entering into the interior castle and closing the door to the outside world for a time in order to commune with one's Higher Self.

16. El Morya, *The Chela and the Path: Keys to Soul Mastery in the Aquarian Age* (Gardiner, Mont.: Summit University Press, 1976), p. 32.
17. Matthew 6:6.

HEART MEDITATION

The following is a short meditation that can help you draw more light and love from your Higher Self into your threefold flame and heart center. You can then send that radiant, positive energy out into the world.

1. Go within and bring your attention to your heart, placing your hand over your heart to draw your awareness there.
2. Close your eyes and breathe deeply several times until you feel calm and centered.
3. Visualize yourself seated before a beautiful altar in the secret chamber of your heart. See a threefold flame blazing upon the altar. Envision yourself robed in garments befitting this holy occasion.
4. Focus on the image of your threefold flame. Visualize large, pulsating blue, golden and pink flames radiating out from the center of your chest. Feel deep love and gratitude in your heart for the gift of life that has been given to you. Now intone the *Aum* as you hold this visualization.
5. Give the following affirmation to increase the flow of light from your Christ Self to your heart and then out into the world.

www.SummitLighthouse.org/SA1-4

I AM THE LIGHT OF THE HEART

I AM the light of the heart
Shining in the darkness of being
And changing all into the golden treasury
Of the mind of Christ.

I AM projecting my love
Out into the world
To erase all errors
And to break down all barriers.

I AM the power of infinite love,
Amplifying itself
Until it is victorious,
World without end!

6. Seal your meditation with the following prayer:

Beloved Holy Christ Self, I ask you to show me how to walk more closely with you each day. Keep my heart pure and attuned to your divine direction at all times. I am grateful for the gift of life and the presence of God within my heart.

> *May God fire the heart with his presence.*[18]
>
> —RALPH WALDO EMERSON

18. Ralph Waldo Emerson, "The Over-Soul," in *Self-Reliance: The Wisdom of Ralph Waldo Emerson as Inspiration for Daily Living,* ed. Richard Whelan (New York: Crown Publishers, 1991), pp. 68–69.

The Power of Dynamic Decrees

Unseen spiritual forces are responsible for the answers to our prayers, both silent and spoken. Here's a look at how heaven responds to our entreaties and to an innovative and powerful form of the spoken Word called the "dynamic decree." By putting a decree to the test for yourself, you can observe its benefits in your daily affairs.

Commanding by the Power of the Word

The power of the spoken Word is well documented. For example, the Bible records that Jesus Christ used the spoken Word to perform many miracles. He commanded the sick to be healed, the stormy wind and sea to be still, and evil spirits to come out of those who were possessed. He even raised a man from the dead through the spoken Word. The Gospel of John records that Jesus cried with a loud voice, "Lazarus, come forth!"[19] and Lazarus arose from the dead, unwinding the grave clothes that bound him.

Jesus

The science of the spoken Word is the most effective method known today for spiritual resolution and progress. The practice of this science distinguishes the teachings of the ascended masters from those of most other organizations. It combines prayer, meditation and visualization with affirmations and dynamic decrees using the name of God, "I AM."

The ascended masters teach that it is necessary to use this powerful tool to counteract the increasing disorder and decay of our time. We see bad news daily about the adverse effects of weather, war and crime. We don't need to feel helpless in the face of these things. Using the science of the spoken Word is a fast, convenient way for us to effect positive change on the planet. By verbally calling to God, the ascended masters and angels, we can become the instruments of heaven on earth and actively help to resolve many negative conditions.

19. John 11:43.

How the Dynamic Decree Commands Heaven's Response

Human beings have traditionally contacted the Supreme Being through prayer. When we pray, we silently or verbally call to God in adoration or thanksgiving. We may confess our wrongdoings or petition him to help us. With prayer, we open ourselves up to communing with Spirit through the desiring of our heart. Once that communion is established, the grace of the Deity descends into our world as light and energy that can effect miraculous change.

Much unseen work of heavenly hosts also occurs in response to our prayers. Betty Eadie, the survivor of a near-death experience, said that from heaven, prayer looks like lights of various sizes shooting up from all over the earth. The size of the light depends upon the strength of the prayer. Some of the lights are tiny, like sparks, and others are big, broad laserlike beams of light. Angels rush to answer the stronger and brighter prayers first and then they answer all the rest.[20]

Because of the power of sound, speaking a prayer out loud has a stronger action than praying silently. The dynamic decree is a carefully worded form of spoken prayer. Decrees differ from regular prayer because the words have been dictated by the ascended masters and contain specific, unique patterns of light. In fact, the words of decrees are sometimes called "cups of light." In a dictation, the Ascended Master Omri-Tas said, "We have released to you in our decrees worded cups of light, mantras out of the pure octaves of Spirit, out of the causal bodies of the ascended masters."[21]

Decrees are the most powerful of all supplications to the Supreme Being. They tap into the limitless power of God by using the name "I AM" just as affirmations do. Simply reciting a decree sets a certain pattern for the light of Spirit to flow into matter. And when given with devotion, the dynamic decree more effectively draws down the light of the I AM Presence to bring about the greatest possible good.

Decrees can command instantaneous action by the hosts of heaven, ascended masters, angels and archangels. Whereas a single prayer may evoke a response from a few angels, a simple decree given with deep devotion and concentration can summon a hundred thousand angels to the side of a person who needs them. The Ascended Master Saint Germain told us that when we give a decree in the full fervor of our hearts, the highest angels of heaven are awakened. The passionate decree appears to them like a fire burning on earth. He said that as soon as such a decree is spoken, bands of angels rush forward to fulfill the command.

20. Betty J. Eadie, *Embraced by the Light* (Placerville, Calif.: Gold Leaf Press, 1992), pp. 103–4.
21. *Pearls of Wisdom,* vol. 31, no. 3, p. 26.

Giving a decree more than once multiplies this effect even further. As the decree is repeated, the sound waves are strengthened and the vibration intensifies. The rhythmic repetition of words sets up cascading waves of power, much like waves of light become amplified in the creation of a laser beam. A laser beam can burn through solid metal. In the same way, a properly produced current of rhythmic sound can transmute physical matter and dissolve density and discord.

> *Remember, many things can change quickly by the alchemy*[22] *of fervent prayer. Prayer is always an alchemy. Your prayers are an alchemy between your soul and your mighty I AM Presence, mediated by your Holy Christ Self and the Holy Spirit.*
>
> *Just so is the divine decree and the science of the spoken Word. Just so is the fiat and the mantra. And each time you engage in the practice of the science of the spoken Word in joy and in love, sending forth your decrees out into the universe, there is a corresponding alchemy of change in your own being.*[23]
>
> —THE ASCENDED MASTER LANELLO

Decrees Are Like Spiritual "Letters"

Decrees can be considered spiritual letters because, like letters, they are composed of three parts: (1) a greeting called the "preamble," (2) the "body" of the decree and (3) the "closing." The characteristics of the body of the decree are outlined below.

The Decree Body

The body of this spiritual letter is a carefully worded formula composed of statements that call forth a spiritual quality to effect positive change for the person decreeing as well as many others. It expresses the desire to become more of one's innate divinity and is a request for help from the Higher Self and the ascended masters. For example, the body of a decree calling upon the cosmic quality of mercy looks like this:

Descending drops of mercy,
Like gentle summer rain,
Melt all hardened substance,
Dissolve my inner pain!

In I AM name!
In I AM name!
In I AM name!

Simply put, the body of the decree contains the command for light's action in the world. This part of the decree can be repeated as many times as desired to increase its effect. The more times it is said, the more light is released to perform the requested action.

22. Alchemy is the ability to change or transmute substance.
23. *Pearls of Wisdom,* vol. 38, no. 37, p. 412.

SPOKEN WORD PRACTICE: EXPERIMENT WITH GIVING A DECREE

Try the following experiment to see how the science of the spoken Word can make a difference in your life. You will be giving the body of a decree called "Introit to the Holy Christ Self."

1. Sit in a comfortable chair in a place where you will not be disturbed.
2. Breathe deeply until you are calm and centered.
3. Give the following decree to help you attune to your Christ Self through your threefold flame, which is also known as your "Holy Christ flame." Give verse one followed by the refrain, verse two followed by the refrain, then verse three followed by the refrain. Repeat this entire sequence three times.

www.SummitLighthouse.org/SA1-5

INTROIT TO THE HOLY CHRIST SELF

1. Holy Christ Self above me,
Thou balance of my soul,
Let thy blessed radiance
Descend and make me whole.

Refrain: Thy flame within me ever blazes,
Thy peace about me ever raises,
Thy love protects and holds me,
Thy dazzling light enfolds me.
I AM thy threefold radiance,
I AM thy living Presence
Expanding, expanding, expanding now.

2. Holy Christ flame within me,
Come expand thy triune light;
Flood my being with the essence
Of the pink, blue, gold and white.

3. Holy lifeline to my Presence,
Friend and brother ever dear,
Let me keep thy holy vigil,
Be thyself in action here.

4. If you have any noticeable experiences when giving this decree, write them down in your journal. These may be physical or visual sensations, or feelings such as joy, happiness and peace.
5. Continue practicing this decree daily for one week, writing down your experiences after each session.

6. At the end of the week, review the notes in your journal. Read the following questions and write a brief summary of any changes you noticed while giving this decree.

   - What are the major effects I have noticed during my practice sessions?
   - Has anything happened during the week that I think may be the result of my having given this decree?

7. Determine how you would like to use this decree in the weeks to come. If you are seeing positive changes, you may wish to continue giving it daily and recording the results.

CHAPTER 3

Living a Spiritual Life in a Material World

Expressing Your Higher Self

With a basic understanding of our Higher Self and the divine spark within the heart as a foundation, let's take a close look at how we express ourselves in the physical world. Mastering the complex energies of our material nature can help us achieve greater harmony in the activities of daily life, express more of our Higher Self and thereby elevate our soul.

Leading a Spiritual Life

It's a fact of life that sometimes it is hard to feel spiritual in a physical body. It's easy to let the physical take precedence over the spiritual. It's easier to let energy gravitate to the density of the material world than it is to raise one's consciousness to spiritual dimensions. In addition to the body, thoughts and emotions are part of the earthly consciousness and everyone deals with them. Anyone who has ever meditated knows what it means to be distracted by the sensations of the body, the persistence of random thoughts and the intrusion of the emotions.

Many meditation teachers direct their pupils to welcome these distractions, to acknowledge them for what they are in order to move beyond them to higher consciousness. In fact, one of the major tests in earth's schoolroom is learning to integrate the energies of Spirit with the energies of matter. Living a truly spiritual life means expressing spirituality in every way—physically, mentally and emotionally. Here's what this entails.

We're Clothed in Four Lower Bodies

The spiritual energies of our higher nature are contained in what the ascended masters call the three "higher bodies": the I AM Presence, the Causal Body and the Holy Christ Self. There are also four "lower bodies," which are the bodies used for expressing ourselves in the material world. These are the physical body, the emotional body, the mental body and the etheric body. The emotional, mental and etheric bodies are composed of matter that vibrates at frequencies higher than physical substance, which makes them invisible to the average human eye. All four lower bodies provide the opportunity for the soul to grow and develop greater self-awareness and mastery through everyday affairs.

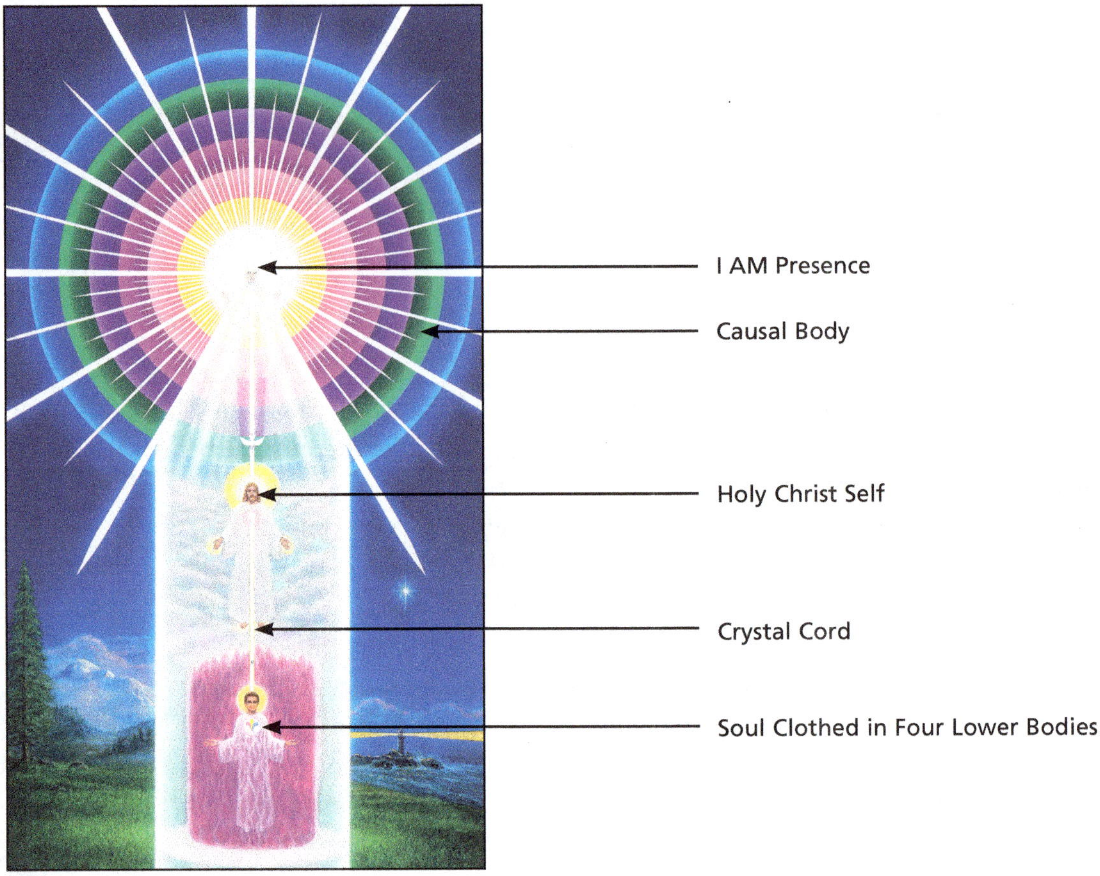

Chart of Your Divine Self

The soul (clothed in the four lower bodies) receives the radiance of the I AM Presence through the Christ Self for the purpose of experiencing matter, for the attainment of self-mastery and for the fulfillment of her divine plan. The soul is the recipient of this divine light because she represents the feminine polarity of being. The Higher Self is the masculine polarity, the light of the Spirit from which the creative energy comes.

The four lower bodies serve a sacred purpose. Because they are the dwelling place of the soul while it is in matter, it is important to understand how to best use them to accelerate one's progress on the spiritual path. Each body has a separate consciousness, yet together they act as a whole, influencing each other. These four lower bodies are vehicles that the soul uses to navigate in the material world. Each body, or vehicle, has a specific function. Each is designed to help facilitate the mission of the soul on earth.

Chapter 2 said that matter is a step-down of spiritual energy that has coalesced in form. Like the higher bodies, the four lower bodies are composed of energy. They can be visualized as sheaths of interpenetrating fields of energy surrounding the soul, with each body vibrating at a different rate. The following chart shows the level of their vibration, from the highest to the lowest.

THE FOUR LOWER BODIES	CORRESPONDING ELEMENTS	LEVEL OF VIBRATION
Etheric	Fire	highest vibrating body
Mental	Air	↓
Emotional	Water	
Physical	Earth	lowest vibrating body

The four lower bodies can be linked to the elements of fire, air, water and earth. In this association, the etheric body corresponds to the fire element, since it permits one to realize God as sacred fire. The mental body can be related to the element of air because of the rapid, changeable nature of thought. The emotional body corresponds to the element of water, which flows constantly like the emotions. The physical body relates to the earth element, since it is used to anchor the light of Spirit in matter.

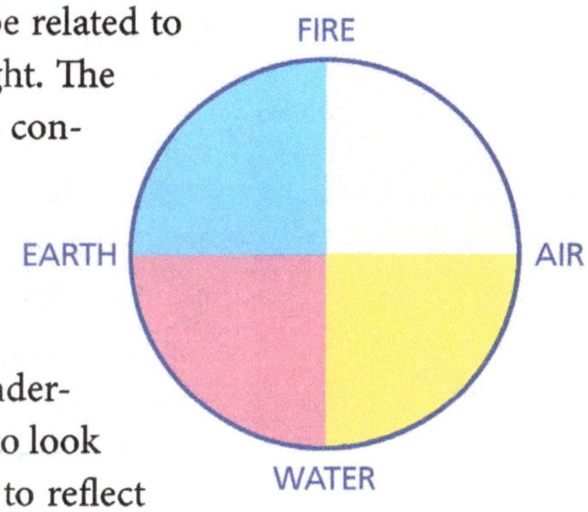

It is possible to raise the vibration of the four lower bodies using the spiritual light of the Higher Self so that they can be the best possible instruments for the soul's development. To gain an understanding of how to master the energies of these bodies, it is helpful to look at their specific functions. As you read about them, you may wish to reflect on how each of these bodies is functioning in your life today.

The Etheric Body

The etheric body, also called the memory body, contains all of one's memories. Memory is critical. It provides the database upon which current choices can be based and it allows the seeker to progress in life. It records everything from a brief moment in our childhood to a deep understanding of who we are in Spirit.

Memory defines identity. In a dictation given in 1967, the Ascended Master Serapis Bey said, "Without memory, identity would fall. Without memory, purpose would not be perceived, nor would there be any integration of purpose. The gift of memory is intended to be a purified faculty designed by God to enable men to rise in awareness, step by step, until self-mastery is gained."[1]

Not only does the etheric body contain the memory of the present lifetime, but it also contains the memory of everything that has transpired since the soul was first created. All of the thoughts, feelings, words and actions that a soul has ever expressed through the mental, emotional and physical bodies are recorded in what is called the lower etheric body. Even if one is not consciously aware of these memories, the soul is aware of them at inner levels.

Everyone has experienced painful memories. These memories can cause fear, anxiety, anger or sadness in the present, even if an incident took place many years or lifetimes ago. Intense memories, including unconscious ones, can also

1. *Pearls of Wisdom,* vol. 10, no. 17, p. 2.

prevent one from experiencing fulfillment and personal growth. Moreover, negative memories can prevent the seeker from fully recognizing his soul's mission.

Because the etheric body is the highest vibrating of the four lower bodies, it is the entryway to the higher bodies. Therefore, it can receive the illumination of the Christ Self most easily and then transmit that light to the other three lower bodies. When the etheric body is cleared of negative memories, one is free to see the single most important memory that God impressed upon the etheric body in the beginning—the memory of the soul's divine blueprint. This blueprint is stored in the higher etheric body and is twofold. It contains: (1) the blueprint of origin—the soul's creation after the image and likeness of God, and (2) the blueprint of the soul's divine plan, which the soul received in the beginning and which she came forth to fulfill in the realms of matter. This divine blueprint is more than four-dimensional and contains the record and nature of the I AM Presence.

The more clearly the seeker sees the inner blueprint, the more likely he will be able to manifest it. And when she fulfills her highest inner potential, the soul experiences joy. So the blueprint is there, but because the etheric body also has scars of past painful experiences, the divine pattern is not always perceived. Later in this chapter, a high-frequency spiritual energy that can literally erase negative memories is discussed. Purification with this alchemical eraser—the violet transmuting flame—can enable one to perceive his inner blueprint more rapidly and move forward to fulfill his divine potential.

The etheric body also serves as a vehicle for soul travel out of the body during sleep, a topic covered extensively in *Sacred Adventure 2: Meeting the Masters.*

The Mental Body

The mental body vibrates at a frequency just below that of the etheric body. The most obvious function of the mental body is to think. It analyzes and organizes information in order to solve problems and draw conclusions about myriad situations in life. A well-functioning mental body is also necessary in order to reason, to concentrate and to communicate clearly and effectively with others. The mental body is developed and strengthened by exercise, much like the physical body. This is done through reading, studying and meditating.

Learning to control and discipline the thought processes is an essential element of the spiritual path. Thought, which operates at unseen energetic levels, is a dynamic and creative force. Therefore, how and what a person thinks can greatly influence the outcome of events in his life. Many spiritual teachers, therapists and self-help authors talk about the power of positive thinking. Thinking positively creates a matrix of energy that can magnetize positive situations. The masters teach us that thoughts can also be destructive and take us off track and far afield from our divine purpose.

The challenge of using the mental body is to sharpen thinking and logic skills while relying on the guidance of the higher mind to give accurate perceptions of reality. This is the way of wisdom. The brain can store all the facts about any number of subjects, yet without wisdom, all the knowledge in the world has limited value. As the book of Proverbs says, "Wisdom is the principal thing; therefore get wisdom, and with all thy getting get understanding."[2]

Study, introspection and analysis combined with the enlightenment of the mind of God bring wisdom and understanding. Wisdom is imparted to the soul through the light of the Christ. This principle was taught by the Gnostics,[3] who believed that the salvation of the soul depended on *gnosis,* the Greek word for knowledge or understanding. In Gnostic works, Jesus is the spiritual teacher and revealer of wisdom who guides the disciple towards self-knowledge. This quest for gnosis involved not only a search for self-knowledge but also for knowledge of God, the cosmos and destiny.

Let this mind be in you, which was also in Christ Jesus.

—PHILIPPIANS 2:5

Such a search requires reaching out beyond the boundaries of the finite mind. It involves accessing the universal mind of God, which is infinite. The way to do this is through the Holy Christ Self, or the Christ consciousness. The mental body is designed to help access that Christ consciousness, which can then provide illumination and divine insights. These insights can bring a heightened awareness of ourselves and our relationship to God and the universe.

A well-functioning mental body is necessary to facilitate this process. It becomes apparent that the mind is much more than the brain, which is simply an instrument that the mind uses to operate in the physical plane. Yet the brain plays a significant role. The right and left hemispheres of the brain are responsible for carrying out the dual function of the mind. While the left brain helps with analysis and logical thinking, the right brain allows access to the intuitive and creative side of the mind. As such, it opens the door to the consciousness of the Christ. When both hemispheres of the brain are balanced, the mental body is stronger. And when strengthened and purified, the mental body is an invaluable aid to progressing on the spiritual path.

We desire man to know that the mind of man is one with the divine mind of God, in like manner that a drop of water is one with the ocean. Possessing the power of reflection, the mind can but examine the Intelligence reflected into it and then, by the processes of reason and analysis, expand that thought by light. When concepts develop into thoughtforms or light patterns they return to the etheric body for storage in the "House of Memory." The brains of men are not their minds, they are but foci through which mental processes operate in the physical realm.[4]

—THE ASCENDED MASTER SERAPIS BEY

---

2. Proverbs 4:7.
3. The Gnostics were a diverse group of Christian sects that flourished mostly in the second and third centuries A.D. The Gnostics claimed to possess an advanced teaching that had been secretly handed down to them from Jesus and his close circle of disciples.
4. Serapis Bey, *Keepers of the Flame Lesson 6* (Gardiner, Mont.: Summit University Press, 1972), p. 17.

The Emotional Body

The emotional body is the body of *e*-nergy in *motion,* or *e-motion.* It is also called the desire body or the astral body. This is the place where feelings are experienced—love, fear, frustration, hope and aspiration. Strong desires or emotions may be experienced as waves of energy that propel one to move into action. People speak of being "moved" when they hear a touching story that expresses deep emotion.

The emotional body enables the soul to perceive the beauty of Spirit in both the visible and invisible worlds. When people experience spiritual feelings such as love, compassion, gratitude and joy, they can share these positive emotions to bring comfort and assistance to others. Looking for the beauty and the divinity within each other makes every person a powerful force for positive change in the world.

The effects of negative emotions can be readily seen in the lives of various individuals and on the world scene—from minor arguments to more destructive behavior. Wars and violence can erupt out of intense feelings of anger, prejudice, hatred and revenge. When people are unable to deal with their emotions, at some level they end up causing harm to themselves or others.

The energy in motion of the emotional body can be the most turbulent and difficult energy to control of all the four lower bodies. Yet mastering that energy brings peace and harmony to the soul and allows her to become a reflecting pool of the beauty and inspiration of her divine Reality.

The Physical Body

The physical body is the vehicle of power and action. It is literally the hands and feet of the other three bodies. Its role in manifesting one's spiritual nature cannot be underestimated. The physical body is the place where one "walks his talk," as they say, and makes his intentions concrete. It can be used to express love for others through speaking kind words or through lending a helping hand, for example.

Using the physical body allows the seeker to bring down to earth the beauty perceived in higher realms. It is used to anchor the light of Spirit in matter. For example, artists use their hands and opera singers use their vocal cords to create works of art that uplift and inspire the hearts and souls of all who see and hear them.

It is easy to see how the physical body correlates with the earth element, as this body is sustained with the fruits of the earth. The physical body is the densest in vibration of the four lower bodies, and the earth is the densest of the four elements. Yet knowing that both the physical body and the earth were created from the energy of Spirit inspires us to treat them with love and respect. The more we imbue our physical bodies and Mother Earth with the energies of Spirit, the more they can help us to carry out our sacred work.

Each of the four lower bodies has the potential to manifest the light and beauty of the soul's spiritual nature, and together they can assist her in her mission. By the same token, impurities or imbalances in these bodies can compromise the soul's ability to make spiritual progress. A look at how these bodies are interrelated may provide a better understanding of the importance of strengthening each of them to create an integrated whole.

Know ye not that ye are the temple of God and that the Spirit of God dwelleth in you?
—I CORINTHIANS 3:16

The Mind-Body-Spirit Connection

Life is full of clear examples of how one body affects another. Being emotionally upset can cause an upset stomach. Worse, continued experiences of stress and agitation may cause a nervous breakdown. Entertaining gloomy thoughts can lead to fear and anxiety, which in turn makes it hard to think clearly.

On the positive side, when people think positive thoughts, they're more inclined to be peaceful and joyful. Being peaceful and harmonious boosts the immune system and makes one less susceptible to illness. Giving recognition to the divine origin of the soul, as recorded in the etheric body, makes one receptive to creative ideas and provides the inspiration to fulfill desired goals.

Studies in the field of mind-body medicine confirm the interrelationship of the mind, body and emotions and examine their impact on each other. For example, numerous clinical studies have shown the positive effects of love and support in preventing cardiovascular disease. Mind-body researchers have shown that when people feel loved, these feelings are translated into biochemical messengers that circulate to the cells and tissues of the body, producing a beneficial result. Researchers have also shown that our positive thoughts have a similar influence on the body.

One study demonstrated the healing effects of individuals' efforts to resolve negative thoughts and feelings associated with traumatic events. The study focused on patients engaged in a process of honest self-examination to release their deepest and most painful thoughts and feelings through writing and talking. Reduced doctors' visits, improved serum immune function and enhanced work performance were some of the observed results.[5] This study showed that energy that has been tied up with negative thoughts, feelings and memories can be moved out of the body. Healing energies can then replace the energy of past traumas.

The ascended masters have explained that most physical diseases originate from disturbances in the etheric, mental and emotional bodies. In a dictation given on October 14, 1973, the Ascended Lady Master Meta said that the etheric body is the body of cause, while the physical body is the body of effect. All that ultimately occurs within the physical body begins as a cause in the memory of man. This initial impulse is then etched upon the mental body and the feeling

5. Taken from a study conducted by Dr. James Pennebaker, professor of psychology and author of *Opening Up: The Healing Power of Confiding in Others* (New York: Avon, 1991) as reported in The Mind/Body Connection website, www.mindbodymed.com/index.html.

body, and manifests finally in the physical form.

When we recognize that the four lower bodies are the vehicles the soul uses to accomplish its spiritual ends, we see how important it is to understand their interrelatedness, and to make an effort to purify and heal them. Balance and harmony are always key elements in making the four lower bodies fitting vehicles for the soul.

The cooperation of all four lower bodies is necessary for success in any undertaking. In fact, each of the bodies has an essential function in all that we do. Consider, for example, the completion of our projects and plans. Any project or goal can be considered as a four-step process that involves each body:

1. The inspiration or idea to initiate a project comes through the etheric body.

2. The mental body is used to think through the details of the project and form a strategy or plan to implement the idea.
3. The desire and motivation to carry the project through to completion are generated through the emotional body.
4. The plan is brought to fruition in the physical plane through the physical body.

Having a weakness in any of the bodies can cause an imbalance and hinder the realization of goals. For example, some people have fantastic ideas, yet because of blockages in the emotional body they may be unable to sustain the desire and passion that would give them the staying power to bring their ideas to fruition. Some people have big hearts and a strong desire to serve others but lack a detail-oriented mind that can translate that desire into a positive plan for action. Looking at our strengths and weaknesses in these areas can help correct any imbalances and lead to more fruitful ventures.

SELF-ASSESSMENT: HOW YOU RELATE TO YOUR FOUR LOWER BODIES

The following exercise can help you assess how you relate to each of your four lower bodies. You may find that one or more of your bodies is predominant over the others. This is the case with most people. The exercise may also reveal areas that you would like to strengthen in order to achieve more balance in your life.

1. On a scale of 1 to 5, where 1 is "never true of me" and 5 is "always true of me," please rate the following statements based on your perception of your life.

1	Never true of me
2	Rarely true of me
3	Sometimes true of me
4	Often true of me
5	Always true of me

a) **How I relate to my physical body:**	1	2	3	4	5
I maintain positive images/thoughts about my body.					
When I am stressed, I take time to unwind.					
I exercise regularly.					
I get adequate rest.					
I live and work in surroundings that are comfortable to me.					
I eat foods that I know are good for me.					

b) **How I relate to my emotional body:**	1	2	3	4	5
When faced with a stressful situation, I remain calm and centered.					
I am open and loving with others.					
As a rule, I follow my gut feelings.					
I nurture myself by doing things that make me happy.					
I remain motivated when working on projects.					
I appreciate the beauty in others and in the world around me.					
I feel joyful and happy much of the time.					

c) **How I relate to my mental body:**	1	2	3	4	5
I think through the pros and cons of an issue before making decisions.					
I like to read and study.					
I comprehend the dynamics of problems and situations.					
When working on a project, I plan all aspects carefully.					
I easily grasp new ideas.					

d) **How I relate to my etheric body:**	1	2	3	4	5
I receive inspiration and come up with new ideas.					
When making decisions, I seek guidance from my Higher Self or a higher power.					
I use what I have learned from the past to direct my actions.					
I am guided by my intuition.					
I believe I am on track in pursuing my mission in life.					

2. Add up your scores for each body. High scores indicate strength in the lower bodies being scored.

3. Take a moment to review your scores. Which lower bodies are your strongest? Which bodies are less well-developed?

4. Formulate several practical steps you can take to strengthen your weaker bodies and to achieve greater balance in all four lower bodies. Write these down in your journal.

Purifying the Four Lower Bodies

We can make the greatest spiritual progress and most easily restore our soul to her original wholeness by purifying and bringing into balance the energies of the four lower bodies. While there are many ways to go about this, including psychotherapy and various healing practices, the ascended masters have given us some marvelous spiritual tools to accelerate the process.[6]

The Healing Light of the I AM Presence

The light of the I AM Presence can help to balance and heal your four lower bodies in a number of ways. Chapter 1 suggested meditating upon the name of God, "I AM THAT I AM," and giving "I AM" affirmations. When given with full faith and devotion, "I AM" affirmations can bring the light of your Presence into whatever situation you are addressing. For instance, if you say, "I AM perfect

6. The light of the I AM Presence and the violet flame, discussed later in this chapter, can indeed facilitate our healing. They are adjuncts to sound medical measures, however, and not a substitute for them. No guarantee whatsoever is made to anyone by The Summit Lighthouse, Summit University, Summit University Press, Mark L. Prophet or Elizabeth Clare Prophet that any aspects of the science of the spoken Word, including decrees, visualization and meditation, will yield successful results for anyone at any time. We always need to be sensible about following the basic laws of health, diet and wholesome living, and consult with medical professionals when necessary. Medical science has much to offer and, if needed, we should pursue traditional medical treatment.

harmony manifesting in my emotional body" or "I AM the clear mind of God acting in this situation," you are affirming that God in you, your mighty I AM Presence, is bringing about the desired condition. In *The "I AM" Discourses,* the Ascended Master Saint Germain says: "Constantly remind the outer consciousness that when you say, 'I AM,' you have set into action *all* the attributes of the Godhead.... When you say, 'I AM' in any condition, it means that instant action is taking place there by the Greatest Power in the Universe. The moment you become conscious that 'I AM' is the Full Activity of God, containing all the attributes of the Godhead, you do that moment have the full use of this Mighty Power."[7]

Calling directly to the heart of your Presence can also produce startling results. There are many stories of students of the ascended masters who have struggled with a problem until they remembered to make a quick call to their I AM Presence. And then, instantaneously, the solution was before them. Whenever you are faced with a challenge, big or small, you can simply say, "Mighty I AM Presence, please help me to [fill in the blank]."

Yet another way to bring the light of your Higher Self into your four lower bodies is through meditation. Focusing your attention on your Presence for a specific purpose, such as that in the meditation below, can produce a powerful harmonizing action for wholeness and balance.

MEDITATION: RADIATING THE LIGHT OF SPIRIT THROUGH YOUR FOUR LOWER BODIES

The following meditation is designed to help you draw down the light of Spirit, the energy of your I AM Presence, and to radiate it through your four lower bodies to cleanse and purify them.

www.SummitLighthouse.org/SA1-6

1. Go within and draw your attention to your heart. You can place your hand over your heart to help focus your awareness there.
2. Breathe deeply until you feel calm and centered.
3. With your eyes closed, chant the words *I AM THAT I AM* nine times.
4. Visualize and feel the divine light of your I AM Presence descending over your crystal cord through your Christ Self into your heart.
5. See and feel that light expanding outward from your heart and penetrating each of your four lower bodies, one at a time.
6. Let the light-energy flow first into your physical body, radiating into every muscle, organ, and cell. Visualize the light flooding and consuming any troublesome physical condition you may have, producing perfect health and vitality.

7. Godfré Ray King, *The "I AM" Discourses* by Saint Germain (Chicago: Saint Germain Press, 1940), p. 57.

7. In your emotional body, let the light of your I AM Presence radiate into any negative feelings you may have. Let it dissolve all anger, frustration, anxiety, fear and grief. Feel it washing over you, eliminating all tension and establishing a profound peace.

8. As the light-energy moves into your mental body, see it penetrate and consume any negative or disturbing thoughts. See these thoughts melting as the light of your Presence moves through them, producing a positive mental outlook.

9. Now, in the etheric body, try to recall a painful memory. Direct the light of your I AM Presence into this remembrance. See it dissolve every facet of the memory until it entirely disappears.

10. Conclude your meditation with the following affirmations:

I AM the perfect wholeness and harmony of my four lower bodies now made manifest! (3x)[8]

I AM grateful for the gift of light in my world today! (3x)

I AM light, light, light! (3x)

The Healing Power of the Violet Flame

Notice that the soul and four lower bodies, represented by the lower figure in the Chart of Your Divine Self, are surrounded by violet-colored flames. These flames depict a high-frequency spiritual energy called the violet flame, which can be invoked by the spoken Word.

Soul in Physical Form

The violet flame acts at subtle energy levels of one's being to consume the negative thoughts, feelings and memories that have accumulated over many lifetimes. Many people who have invoked this transforming energy have seen dramatic changes—physically, mentally, emotionally and spiritually—when they have used it regularly.

When the violet flame clears the etheric body of its negative memories and impressions, the original perfection of the divine blueprint can shine through. The soul is then able to see her divine plan more clearly. As the four lower bodies are purified, they become clearer vessels to receive the light of the Holy Christ Self. And as the individual embodies more of the Christ consciousness, he becomes a fountain of blessing and healing to other parts of life. The "Liberating Power of the Word" section that follows explains more about the qualities of this purifying energy and how invoking it can bring about seemingly miraculous results.

8. "3x" in affirmations and decrees means to give the line or stanza three times.

The Violet Transmuting Flame

The marvelous sacred energy of the violet transmuting flame can help purify the four lower bodies and help the soul fulfill her mission. This section launches the use of this transformative, spiritual elixir. But before we consider in greater detail how the violet flame works, it's good to have a deeper understanding of the characteristics of dynamic decrees and how to get the maximum benefit from the science of the spoken Word.

The Opening and Closing of a Decree

Chapter 2 mentioned the three parts of a decree: the preamble, the body and the closing, and covered the characteristics of the decree body. This section discusses the preamble and the closing of the dynamic decree in more depth.

The Preamble

The preamble of any decree is like the salutation of a letter—it tells to whom the decree is addressed. Decrees are given in the name of the I AM Presence and Holy Christ Self. When we call upon our own Higher Self, we are tapping into our full God-potential. We can also call to the Holy Christ Self of all mankind to reinforce this action.

You may call to specific ascended masters or angels to help bring about the given request, as well. The preamble of each decree names key spiritual beings through whose hearts flow an extraordinary momentum of the particular quality or virtue expressed in the body of the decree. These beings are major giving and receiving centers of that light, and they are always willing to grant us the divine qualities we request when the energy is used for positive purposes. For example, if you are praying for protection, it might be helpful to name Archangel Michael in the preamble, since he is an archangel of protection.

According to cosmic law, the call compels the answer. The ascended masters have explained that when we call to them with devotion in the name of our I AM Presence and Holy Christ Self, they must come spiritually to us. The Ascended Master Saint Germain says that the process is just as sure as when you get on the phone and call the fire department or ring the fire alarm. Out come the fire engines and they rush to the place where you've called them. In the same way, the masters come when you call. They are never too busy to help. When they come, they manifest the perfection of the quality that you invoke. So if you call to a master for the cosmic quality of mercy, he or she can be counted upon to release that quality.

Here is an example of a decree preamble:

> "In the name of the beloved mighty victorious Presence of God, I AM in me, my very own beloved Holy Christ Self, Holy Christ Selves of all mankind and beloved Archangel Michael, I decree . . . "

The preamble is then followed by the body of the decree.

The Closing

The closing of the decree represents your acceptance that your "letter" has been received in the heart of God. It seals the action of precipitation that causes light from Spirit to descend tangibly into matter. It is the moment when we announce to the universe that the decree that we have given will become physical in our life. Most decrees use the following formal closing:

> And in full faith I consciously accept this manifest, manifest, manifest! (3x) right here and now with full power, eternally sustained, all-powerfully active, ever expanding and world enfolding until all are wholly ascended in the light and free!
>
> Beloved I AM! Beloved I AM! Beloved I AM!

The closing and the preamble are extremely powerful parts of the decree. It is therefore important to include both when giving decrees. You will have the opportunity to give the preamble, the body of the decree and the closing to invoke the violet flame later in this section.

The Violet Flame Transmutes Negativity

Let's take a closer look at the violet flame. The violet flame is a special cosmic light introduced to us by the Ascended Master Saint Germain. As mentioned earlier, it is a wonderful tool that helps clear the mind, free the emotions and heal the body. By invoking the violet flame in decrees, one's soul can more quickly reunite with her Holy Christ Self and fulfill her reason for being.

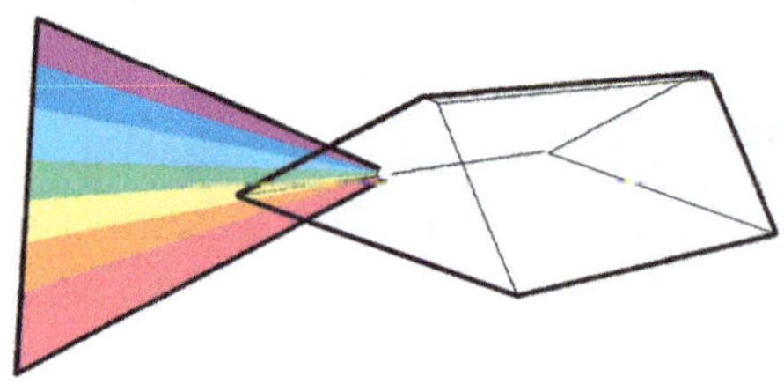

Just as the white light of the sun is refracted into the seven colors of the rainbow, the pure light of the I AM Presence manifests as seven spiritual rays. These rays comprise the spheres of the causal body surrounding the I AM Presence. Each of these spiritual rays has a specific color and frequency as well as its own unique qualities.

Causal Body

The divine energy of any of the spiritual rays turns into a "flame" when we call it into action through the spoken Word. This process can be compared to the way sunlight passing through a magnifying glass creates a physical flame.

The violet flame is a high-frequency spiritual light that descends to the soul over the crystal cord from the violet sphere of the causal body. The specific frequency of the violet ray conveys the action of mercy, justice, freedom and transmutation. Transmutation is the process of changing something into a higher form. So the vibration of the violet flame has the capacity to transmute the impure elements of the four lower bodies into a vibration more closely resembling that of the Higher Self.

With regular use, the violet flame can bring about transformation at all levels of being. It can enhance stamina and help to overcome physical problems and emotional hang-ups. It can lift the spirit and free the soul to pursue her divine plan. The masters call the violet flame a universal solvent because of its wondrous ability to dissolve problems at subtle energy levels.

The Violet Flame

The violet flame can especially help with the material concerns we face each day. The Ascended Master Saint Germain said, "The violet flame is the supreme antidote for physical problems." He explained that the violet flame has the ability to change physical conditions because, of all the spiritual frequencies, the violet is closest in vibratory action to the components of matter. "The violet flame can combine with any molecule or molecular structure, any particle of matter known or unknown, and any wave of light, electrons or electricity," he says. "Wherever [people] gather to give the violet flame, there you notice immediately an improvement in *physical* conditions!"[9]

We can direct the violet flame into disease, stress, relationships or any undesirable condition. Sometimes resolution is fast and sometimes it is the result of a gradual process of change. But it works either way, as long as we put forth sincere effort and use the violet flame on a regular basis.

How Does the Violet Flame Work?

Experts in the ancient Oriental art of Feng Shui teach that clutter and the arrangement of the environment determine the flow of energy in our surroundings. If the arrangement is harmonious, the energy flows freely. If the arrangement is inharmonious, the energy is blocked. This flow of energy affects one's health, abundance and relationships.

Similarly, energy constantly flows to us from the I AM Presence and this flow can be blocked or enhanced by our thoughts, words and deeds. Clutter in the body, mind and emotions can cause our energy to stagnate. All of us have some clutter in the four lower bodies. While we have done much good in our lifetimes,

9. *Pearls of Wisdom,* vol. 27, no. 61, p. 553.

we have also created negative karma, the result of wrong thoughts and deeds. This energy has collected and solidified in our physical, mental and emotional worlds. It sticks to the lower bodies like mud. When they are caked with the debris of negative karma, we don't feel as happy, vibrant and spiritual as we could.

The violet flame can literally transmute this karmic "debris." When we invoke the violet flame through decrees, it surrounds each one of our atoms. A polarity is set up between the nucleus of the atom and the violet flame. The nucleus, being matter, assumes the negative polarity; the core of the violet flame, being Spirit, assumes the positive polarity.

Sub-Atomic Violet Flame Action

The interaction between the nucleus of the atom and the light of the violet flame establishes an oscillation, a rapid back and forth movement. This brisk interchange releases the density trapped between the electrons orbiting the nucleus. As this substance is freed, the electrons move more freely and the negative substance is thrown into the violet flame. On contact with the flame, the karmic debris is transmuted and the light-energy is restored to its native purity. It is then returned to the causal body, where it is stored in the concentric spheres of light as one's spiritual treasure. The soul is then able to more effectively pursue her mission and reunite with her Holy Christ Self through her path of progressive spiritual development.

> *Every day in every way the violet flame flushes out and renews your body cells, the cells of your mind, and the globule of your soul, polishing the jewel of consciousness until it glistens in the sunlight.*[10]
>
> —THE ASCENDED MASTER EL MORYA

Invoking the Violet Flame through Decrees

Soul in Physical Form

Giving decrees to the violet flame produces a very uplifting sensation. It is like getting a taste of freedom—liberation from lack, pain and worry. Once most people feel the action of the violet flame in their consciousness and four lower bodies, they want more and more of it.

The violet cylinder surrounding the person in the lower figure of the Chart of Your Divine Self represents you standing in the violet flame. When you give decrees to the violet flame, you begin the process of transmutation that cleanses the four lower bodies and purifies the soul. This action helps you move closer to reunion with your Holy Christ Self. Try the following exercise using the violet flame and see for yourself how good you feel after doing it.

10. El Morya, *The Chela and the Path: Keys to Soul Mastery in the Aquarian Age* (Gardiner, Mont.: Summit University Press, 1976), p. 49.

SPOKEN WORD PRACTICE: "I AM THE VIOLET FLAME"

1. Sit in a comfortable chair in a place where you will not be disturbed.
2. Breathe deeply until you are calm and relaxed.
3. Focus your awareness on your heart, placing your hand over your heart to direct your attention there.
4. Give the following decree to the violet flame. Repeat the body of the decree three times to increase the effect.

I AM THE VIOLET FLAME

(Preamble)

In the name of the beloved mighty victorious Presence of God, I AM in me, my very own beloved Holy Christ Self and Holy Christ Selves of all mankind, I decree:

(Decree Body)

I AM the violet flame
In action in me now
I AM the violet flame
To light alone I bow
I AM the violet flame
In mighty cosmic power
I AM the light of God
Shining every hour
I AM the violet flame
Blazing like a sun
I AM God's sacred power
Freeing every one

(Closing)

And in full faith I consciously accept this manifest, manifest, manifest! (3x) **right here and now with full power, eternally sustained, all-powerfully active, ever expanding and world enfolding until all are wholly ascended in the light and free!**

Beloved I AM! Beloved I AM! Beloved I AM!

www.SummitLighthouse.org/SA1-7

5. Note in your journal any positive changes you experience in your four lower bodies.

CHAPTER 4

Expanding the Flow of Light Within

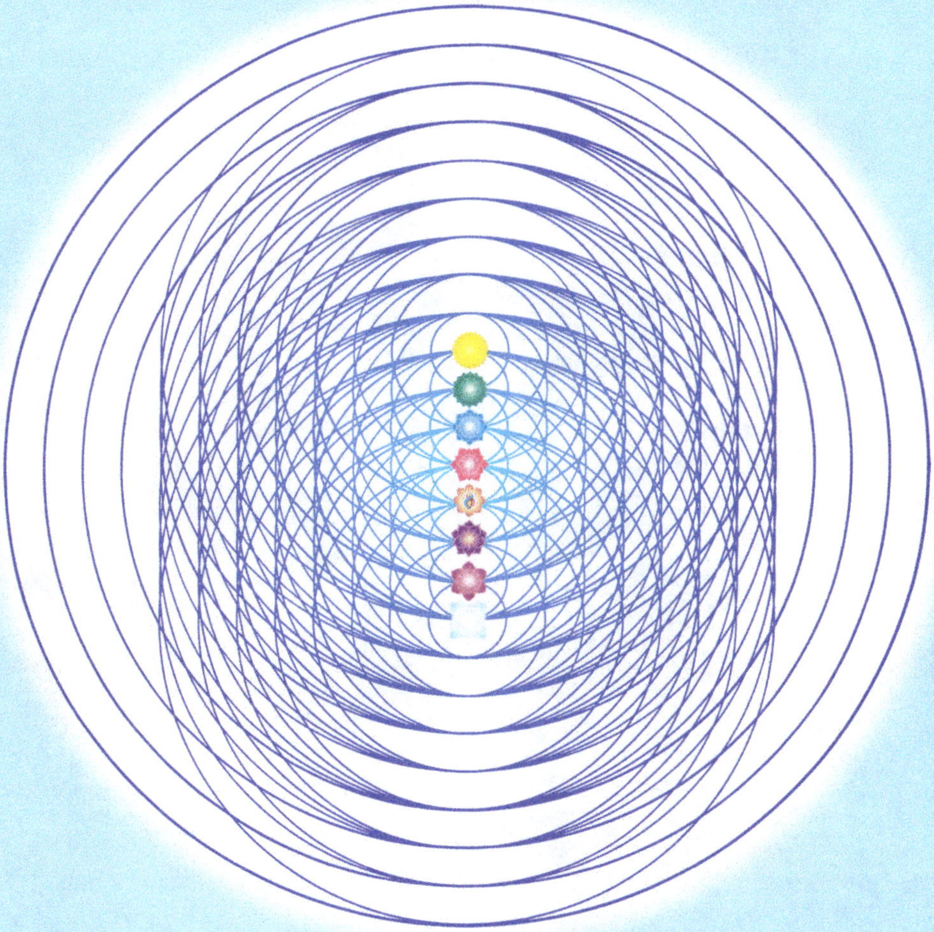

Your Chakras and Aura

Up to this point, we've examined our spiritual make-up, including the origin and blueprint of our divine nature, as well as the components of our Higher Self. We have also looked at the roles of the four different bodies that we use in our physical journey through time and space. Now let's take an in-depth look at the spiritual anatomy of these lower bodies, discover how our spiritual centers (or chakras) work, and learn how the flow of light within us influences our aura and daily activities.

Such understanding can help us further balance and strengthen our etheric, mental, emotional and physical bodies, and expand the flow of the life force within to more fully express our inherent divinity. This in turn will help us draw closer to the ultimate goal of reuniting with our I AM Presence in the ritual of the ascension.

How Light and Life Flow within Us

Here's a quick review of the Chart of Your Divine Self to reiterate how spiritual energy flows to us. The lower figure in this chart represents the soul evolving in matter. Situated above the soul in spiritual dimensions is the source of our divinity, the I AM Presence. A stream of radiant light-energy, or life force, flows to us from our I AM Presence over the crystal cord every moment of our lives.

Chart of Your Divine Self

As this life force flows over the crystal cord, it passes through the Holy Christ Self. The Christ Self, in its great wisdom, steps down the intensity of this powerful spiritual light-energy and regulates it to meet our daily and hourly needs.

The life force enters the body at the top of the head. From there it flows into a complex network of energy distribution stations and channels to sustain life here in the physical world. The most important elements of this distribution system are the spiritual centers called "chakras."

The Chakras—Whirling Vortices of Light

Chakra is a Sanskrit word that means "wheel" or "disc." Chakras are pulsating, dynamic light-energy centers within us that supply the four lower bodies with the subtle energy they need to perform their daily tasks.

Seven Energy Centers

Since the chakras are in the etheric (or memory) body, they can only be seen by those with spiritual sight. Indian yogis and sages who clairvoyantly studied the body's spiritual centers called them "chakras," or "wheels," because the patterns of light they saw radiating out from a central core reminded them of the spokes of a turning wheel. Others who observed these same light-emanations thought that the chakras had a certain resemblance to blossoming lotus flowers. So these seers spoke of the chakras as *padmas,* or "lotuses," and referred to the light-emanations from the core of the chakras as "petals."

Hindu sources usually refer to seven or eight principal chakras. In the ancient Indian tradition, the chakras are seen as repositories and distribution points for prana, the vital force that flows through the body over a network of thousands of threadlike energy channels called *nadis.* Acupuncture and other ancient and new age healing techniques are based on the energy flow along these channels or meridians.

The ascended masters teach that the body has a total of 144 chakras of different sizes and various functions. The chakras are located in the etheric body and govern the flow of energy to the mental, emotional and physical bodies. Seven of them, located along the spine and in the head, are considered the major chakras. These seven major chakras each vibrate at a different rate or frequency and manifest as seven different colors. These seven colors correlate with what are known as the seven rays of spiritual light.

The Beautiful You—the Seven Rays and Chakras

As explained previously, pure light-energy emanates from the Godhead. When this white light passes through the prism of the universal Christ consciousness, it splits into seven spiritual rays in much the same way that sunlight passing through a prism separates into the seven colors of the visible light spectrum.

Each of these seven spiritual rays embodies unique qualities of the Christ consciousness, symbolized by its color. While each ray has many shades of color and meaning, its main characteristics can be captured in one or two words. The colors and primary qualities of the seven rays are shown in the table on the next page.

THE SEVEN RAYS		
RAY	COLOR	QUALITY
First Ray	Blue	Power
Second Ray	Yellow	Wisdom
Third Ray	Pink	Love
Fourth Ray	White	Purity
Fifth Ray	Green	Wholeness
Sixth Ray	Purple and gold flecked with ruby	Service
Seventh Ray	Violet	Freedom

Just how do these seven rays relate to us as spiritual and material beings? As the upper figure in the Chart of Your Divine Self (see p. 57) shows, the causal body is comprised of seven colored energy bands. These bands of light surrounding the I AM Presence contain the light of the seven rays. They show how much divine consciousness we have acquired on each ray and determine how much spiritual energy on that ray is available for us to use in our daily lives.

Just as the bands of our causal body store and release these rays of spiritual light, so the seven major chakras contain and distribute the energy of the seven rays to our four lower bodies. Ideally, as we work with the different chakras and the light that flows through them, we internalize the qualities and virtues of these beautiful emanations of the universal Spirit. Our chakras grow in size and brightness as we absorb these seven rays and make their qualities an integral part of our lives.

Chakras—Their Unique Shapes and Frequencies

Besides having a distinguishing color, each chakra has a unique shape determined by the number of its light-emanations, or "petals." The number of petals varies according to the vibratory rate of the chakra. The lowest vibratory rate is found in the root chakra at the base of the spine, which has four petals. The frequency of the chakras situated higher along the spine increases progressively from the base to the crown, as does the number of petals. So the crown chakra, at the top of the head, has the highest frequency and the most petals. The crown has traditionally been referred to as the thousand-petaled lotus—a close approximation to its amazing 972 petals. In Western religious art, this chakra is frequently depicted as a halo.

The Seven Chakras chart gives a concise overview of the seven major chakras from the top of the head to the base of the spine. It displays the unique characteristics of each chakra: the shape, original Sanskrit name, approximate location in the body, color, number of petals, related spiritual ray and dominant qualities.

THE SEVEN CHAKRAS							
CHAKRA	CROWN	THIRD EYE	THROAT	HEART	SOLAR PLEXUS	SEAT OF THE SOUL	BASE OF THE SPINE

SANSKRIT NAME	Sahasrara	Ajna	Vishuddha	Anahata	Manipura	Svadhishthana	Muladhara
LOCATION	Top of the head	Forehead, between the eyebrows	Throat	Heart	Navel and stomach	Midway between the navel and the base of the spine	Base of the spine
COLOR	Yellow	Green	Blue	Pink	Purple and gold with ruby	Violet	White
PETALS	972	96	16	12	10	6	4
RAY	Second Ray	Fifth Ray	First Ray	Third Ray	Sixth Ray	Seventh Ray	Fourth Ray
QUALITIES	Wisdom Discernment Enlightenment	Wholeness Vision Truth	Power Divine Will Protection	Love Compassion Charity	Service Peace Ministration	Freedom Transmutation Mercy	Purity Order Discipline

The chakra colors shown in this chart represent the purest, most etheric emanations of the chakras seen at the deepest spiritual levels. Other esoteric schools give different colors for the seven chakras. The difference may be because clairvoyants who have observed the chakras and codified their colors have not glimpsed these pure manifestations, resulting in other color classifications.

People's chakras are in diverse stages of spiritual development. So the chakras of most individuals are subject to various impurities—something that's discussed a little later. The result is that the chakras of the majority of people will have variances in color and be of differing sizes and brightness.

> *When quite undeveloped [the chakras] appear as small circles about two inches in diameter, glowing dully in the ordinary man; but when awakened and vivified they are seen as blazing, coruscating [light-emitting] whirlpools, much increased in size, and resembling miniature suns.*[1]
>
> —C. W. LEADBEATER

SELF-REFLECTION: THE SEVEN CHAKRAS

Light and energy can flow more freely within one's being when all of the chakras are equally expanded. However, the chakras are not usually equally developed, because we have natural preferences for using some chakras while neglecting others. As a clue to which ones you might prefer, ask yourself the following questions while looking again at The Seven Chakras chart. Write the answers down in your journal.

1. Which chakra colors appeal to me most? Which appeal to me least?
2. Which chakra qualities do I like best? Which appeal to me least?
3. Which qualities do I know I have? Which qualities do I know I need to develop more fully?
4. Write down any further reflections you may have in your journal.

This exercise can not only give you hints as to why some areas of your life are easier than others, but it might also provide you with the motivation to develop areas of your consciousness that you find more challenging.

1. C. W. Leadbeater, *The Chakras,* rev. ed. (Wheaton, Ill.: The Theosophical Publishing House, 1994), p. 4.

Other Chakras

Besides the seven major chakras, there are several other chakras that play prominent roles in the flow of life's energy to us. One of these is the secret chamber of the heart that is the location of the threefold flame. The secret chamber of the heart is the place we go in consciousness when seeking deep communion with sacredness, with the Holy Spirit, with the divine consciousness within all life.

This chakra is also called the secondary heart chamber. It has eight petals and its color is peach, a beautiful blending of pink and gold. The secret chamber of the heart is the focal point for the eighth ray, which is known as the ray of integration. Whereas the seven rays teach us the seven major qualities of the universal Christ consciousness, the eighth ray takes us to the level of integration with that Christ consciousness and ultimately with the I AM Presence. This eighth-ray chakra is therefore an important focus for all those on a path of spiritual development.

Secret Chamber of the Heart

As Elizabeth Clare Prophet explained, God has given us an altar, the eighth-ray chakra in the secret chamber of the heart. The soul can go there and commune with Christ and with Buddha. The secret chamber of the heart is a dimension as vast as the whole cosmos, even though it isn't measurable in the physical sense of the word. But spiritually speaking, it is our interior castle, as Teresa of Avila called it. It's the place where we meet our master, our guru, our God and our own Real Self.

There are also five chakras known as the secret-ray chakras. The five secret rays are hidden rays whose colors have not been released to us by the masters. In the upper figure of the Chart of Your Divine Self, the secret rays are hidden in the white-fire core around the I AM Presence in the center of the causal body. The chakras through which we express the secret rays are located in the hands, the feet and the left side of the chest. It is interesting to note that when Jesus was crucified, the physical location of each of his secret ray chakras was pierced, either with nails or a sword.

The secret rays, though called minor rays, play an important role in our spiritual development. The Ascended Master Mighty Cosmos put it succinctly: "The secret rays promote an action of detail, the final sculpturing of the mind and consciousness in the perfect image of the Christ. [They] are like the refiner's fire. They purge, they purify.... [The secret rays] draw all into the plumb line of divinity."[2]

The Human Aura—an Ever-Changing Light Show

Chakras can look like flowers moving gracefully as the wind blows gently through their petals. They are not static points of light. They are dynamic energy centers that constantly take in and send out the spiritual light that flows through our four lower bodies. The Ascended Master Djwal Kul compared this to the

2. *Pearls of Wisdom,* vol. 16, no. 45.

breathing process: "Just as you breathe in and breathe out through the throat chakra, so all of the chakras are taking in and giving forth the energies of God according to the frequency assigned to each specific chakra."[3]

As light streams forth from the chakras, it forms a radiating energy field that penetrates and extends beyond the boundaries of one's physical form. This energy field is commonly called the aura. Researchers have also used other names for different manifestations of the aura, such as L-field (Life field) or T-field (Thought field).

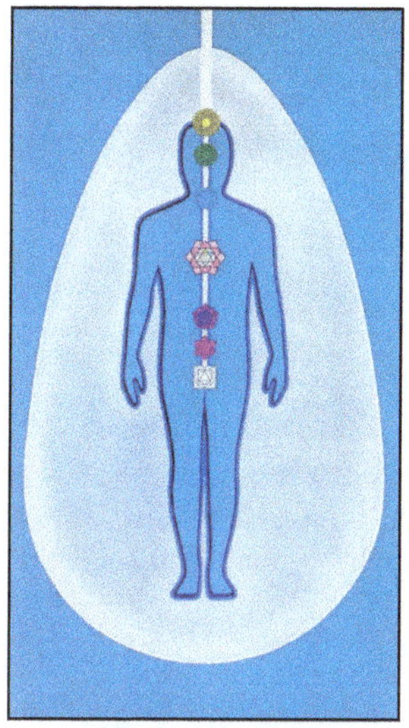
The Human Aura

The aura is actually an ever-changing, multicolored forcefield that reflects the momentary emanations of the chakras as energy passes through them. For instance, when one is engaged in intense thinking, studying or lecturing, an observer whose inner sight is opened would see strong yellow and green emanations coming forth from the crown and third-eye chakras and dominating the area of the aura around the head. At other moments, the same observer could see flashes of pink around the torso when an individual is extending the love of her heart to another. Kirlian photography has been used to capture these color emanations on film. Computer software programs have also been developed that allow one's aura to be seen on a monitor and printed out in picture form.

In *The Human Aura,* the Ascended Master Kuthumi writes concerning the aura: "Each individual in whom is the flame of life reveals himself as though he were to shout it from the housetops—all that he really is, all that he has done, and even the portent of that which he shall be—right in the forcefield of his being and in the magnetic emanations surrounding his physical form."[4] So the energy within the aura carries the vibration of our divine blueprint as well as of all our uses of the light-energy that flows to us.

We may not all be able to see auras, but our souls can take an "inner reading" of this forcefield. For instance, it is easy to sense the difference in the aura of someone who is angry and the aura of someone who is peaceful. The energy is tangibly different to our soul faculties. If you think you do not sense others' auras, try to recall being at a gathering where you didn't really know many people. Perhaps it was at a party, starting the first day of school or beginning a new job. Then remember how within a few short minutes of looking around you could tell which people you might like to get to know and which ones you would prefer to avoid. We often make such decisions by taking an inner, soul reading of people's auras.

Animals can also sense people's auras and tell whether they are emitting fear and hatred or peace and love. That is why Saint Francis could easily befriend otherwise dangerous animals—they were disarmed by the love in his aura.

People can be similarly drawn to other people because of their auras. When the radiation from a person's chakras is pure and harmonious, his aura shines

3. Kuthumi and Djwal Kul, *The Human Aura: How to Activate and Energize Your Aura and Chakras* (Gardiner, Mont.: Summit University Press, 1996), pp. 201, 204.
4. Ibid., p. 3.

forth as a beautiful, luminous, egg-shaped forcefield. It stretches above his head and below his feet and encompasses his four lower bodies, as shown in the color figure on p. 63. It is an energy field of lovely light that blesses others and causes like-minded people to want to be in the presence of such a person.

> *Day by day as the aspirant gains control of the flow of life through his being, the inflow and the outflow of the life forces in the chakras increase until the [moment] when all of the seven chakras, together with the secondary heart chamber, are simultaneously releasing the color rings of the seven rays and the eighth ray from the base of the spine to the crown.*[5]
>
> —THE ASCENDED MASTER DJWAL KUL

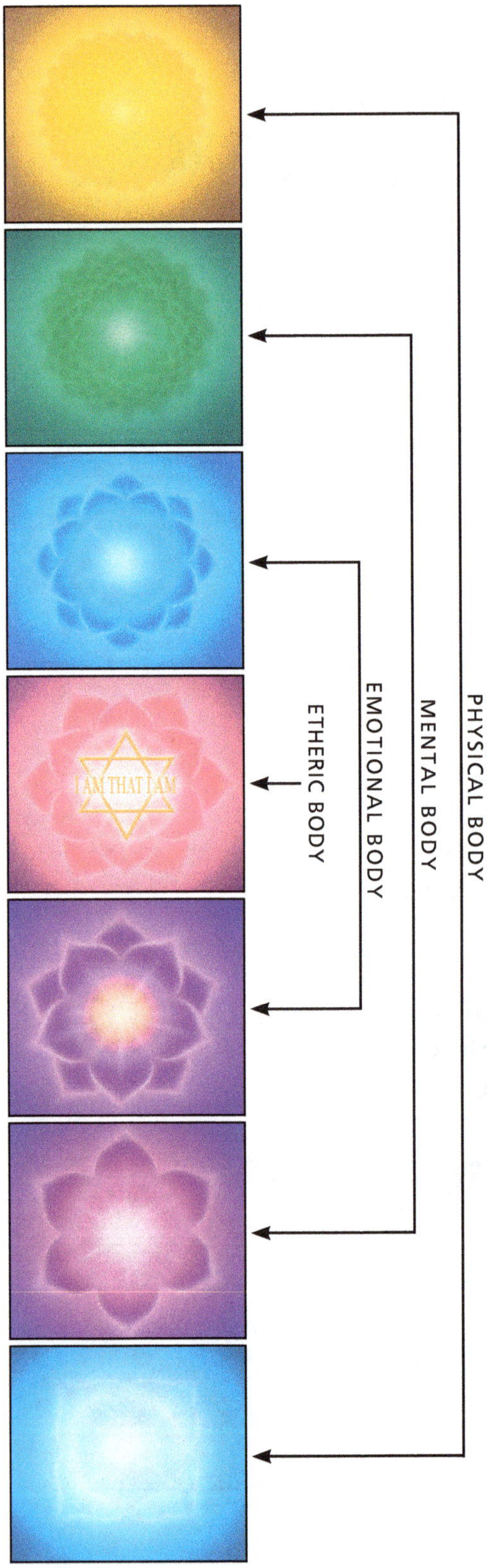

Chakra Pairs

The Distribution of the Life Force

When pure light-energy streams to us from our I AM Presence over the crystal cord, it enters at the crown and then flows to the heart chakra. The heart chakra is the largest of the seven chakras and acts as the main distribution center for the life force that flows to us. From our heart chakra, the energy is distributed to the other chakras. These chakras then release the life force to our four lower bodies. As it reaches the physical body, it courses through the nerve channels to infuse the organs and cells with the spiritual energy necessary to sustain life. Understanding this intricate process of energy flow helps us comprehend how, knowingly or unknowingly, we constantly participate in the process of creating and re-creating ourselves. This is covered more fully in chapter 5.

Part of the dynamics of energy flow in the chakras is that they work in pairs, with a pair consisting of one chakra above and one below the heart. For instance, you may experience butterflies in your stomach before giving a speech, showing the interconnectedness of the throat and solar plexus chakras. Different chakras also have special connections to one of the four lower bodies. These dynamics are outlined in the diagram.

5. Ibid., p. 234.

SPOKEN WORD PRACTICE: INTERIOR HOUSECLEANING—A CHAKRA CLEARANCE

Your chakras are open doors to higher consciousness—if they are clear and vibrate at their intended spiritual frequency. The following affirmations can help you cleanse and accelerate your chakras by saturating them with the violet flame. The affirmation sequence begins with your heart chakra and then weaves through the chakra pairs above and below the heart until all of the seven chakras are bathed in violet fire.

1. Center in your heart and calm your breathing.
2. Look at the picture of the chakras and take a moment to visualize each chakra at its proper place in your body. Impress in your mind the color, shape and the general outline of its petals.
3. Give each of the following mantras three times each, visualizing each chakra filled with a blazing violet flame that transmutes all impurity.

www.SummitLighthouse.org/SA1-8

I AM a being of violet fire,
I AM the purity God desires!

My heart is a chakra of violet fire,
My heart is the purity God desires!

I AM a being of violet fire,
I AM the purity God desires!

My throat chakra is a wheel of violet fire,
My throat chakra is the purity God desires!

I AM a being of violet fire,
I AM the purity God desires!

My solar plexus is a sun of violet fire,
My solar plexus is the purity God desires!

I AM a being of violet fire,
I AM the purity God desires!

My third eye is a center of violet fire,
My third eye is the purity God desires!

I AM a being of violet fire,
I AM the purity God desires!

My soul chakra is a sphere of violet fire,
My soul is the purity God desires!

I AM a being of violet fire,
I AM the purity God desires!

Seven Energy Centers

My crown chakra is a lotus of violet fire,
My crown chakra is the purity God desires!

I AM a being of violet fire,
I AM the purity God desires!

My base chakra is a fount of violet fire,
My base chakra is the purity God desires!

I AM a being of violet fire,
I AM the purity God desires!

4. Intone the *Aum* to seal your meditation.

Preparing the Chakras for Raising Up the Mother Light

The main energy flow covered thus far is the light-energy that descends from the Higher Self over the crystal cord to the Holy Christ Self, then down through the soul's chakras and out into the four lower bodies. Another pattern of energy flow within us is the raising up of light-energy from the base-of-the-spine chakra to the crown chakra.

The base-of-the-spine chakra is a fascinating energy center. The white light that characterizes this chakra is described by the ascended masters as the Mother light, or the sacred fire of the Divine Mother. This sacred fire is life-giving and has tremendous creative power—the power to procreate as well as the power to re-create ourselves.

Hinduism refers to this Mother light as the kundalini; the word *kundalini* literally means "coiled-up serpent." It refers to a powerful, coiled energy in the base chakra that is latent, or "sleeping," in most people. When the kundalini is "awakened," it begins to rise, penetrating and activating each of the chakras along the spine until it reaches the crown chakra.

This white light of the Divine Mother in the base chakra polarizes with the light of the Divine Father in the crown chakra and the two are naturally drawn to each other. So when the light of the I AM Presence descending through the crown chakra and the ascending light of the base chakra meet in the heart chakra, the forces of Father and Mother join together. There, in the cradle of the heart, the Father and Mother give birth to the Christ consciousness within us. In fact,

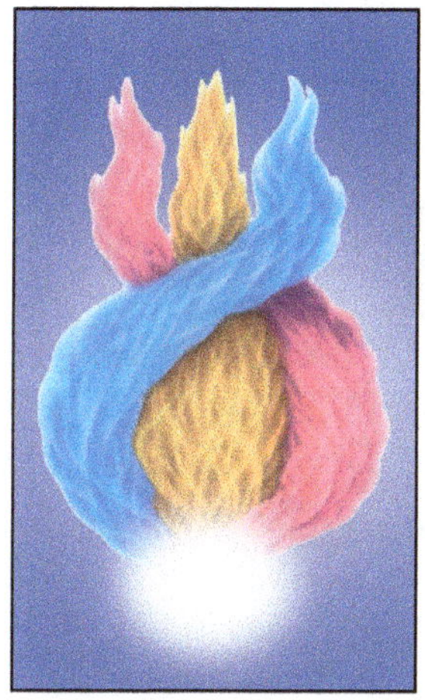

Elizabeth Clare Prophet has said that this union of the energy of the Father-Mother God in our hearts is necessary for us to become the full manifestation of what we are intended to be.

The threefold flame in the heart is also referred to as the Christ flame. This flame is the spiritual fire that focuses the Christ consciousness. The acceleration of the heart chakra as it is touched by the rising kundalini helps the Christ consciousness to blossom within us. After this occurs, the light keeps rising within our chakras. The final stages of the raising of the kundalini take this powerful energy all the way to the crown chakra. When it quickens the crown, the blossoming of the Buddhic consciousness in that center manifests as enlightenment.

> *As long as the mind is attached to the things of this world, it remains in the three lower centers.... While there, it has no higher ambitions and no visions. It is plunged in the passions of lust and greed.*
>
> *The fourth center is the heart. When the mind learns to dwell there, a man has his first spiritual awakening. He has the vision of light all around him. Seeing this light, he marvels and cries: "Ah, what joy!" After this, his mind does not go back to the lower centers.*
>
> *The fifth center is at the throat. When a man's mind reaches that, it is set free from ignorance and delusion. The man does not care to hear or talk of anything but God.*
>
> *The sixth center is at the forehead.... When the mind reaches this center, it has direct vision of God, by day and by night. But, even so, there is a little trace of egotism left.... It's like a light in a lantern. You feel as if you could touch the light but you can't, because the glass prevents you.*
>
> *The seventh center is at the top of the head. When the mind reaches it, it achieves samadhi [enlightenment]. Then one becomes a knower of Brahman [God]. One is united with Brahman [God].*[6]
>
> —RAMAKRISHNA

Raising up the kundalini has been traditionally associated with the acquiring of spiritual powers, called *siddhis* in Hinduism. Examples of siddhis are clairvoyance, clairaudience, the power to materialize objects and the ability to make oneself invisible, fly through the air or walk through fire unharmed. In the desire to acquire these powers some students of the occult sciences try to force the kundalini to rise and awaken their higher chakras.

Many enlightened teachers and gurus, including the ascended masters and their messengers, strongly caution against attempting to awaken the serpent fire

6. Christopher Isherwood, *Ramakrishna and His Disciples* (Hollywood, Calif.: Vedanta Press, 1965), pp. 63–64.

prematurely. They speak about the tremendous creative power locked in the kundalini that may not be easy to control once fully aroused. And they explain that when this fire rises up through chakras that are not yet purified, it contacts the impure energy and magnifies it—sometimes to such an extent that the student is unable to deal with the consequences. An uncontrolled rising of the kundalini may cause physical pain as well as psychological problems. In extreme cases, it may even lead to insanity.

> *The premature unfoldment of the higher aspects of kundalini . . . intensifies everything in the man's nature, and it reaches the lower and evil qualities more readily than the good. In the mental body, for example, ambition is very quickly aroused, and soon swells to an incredibly inordinate degree. It would be likely to bring with it a great intensification of the power of intellect, but at the same time it would produce abnormal and satanic pride, such as is quite inconceivable to the ordinary man. It is not wise for a man to think that he is prepared to cope with any force that may arise within his body; this is no ordinary energy, but something resistless.*[7]
>
> —C. W. LEADBEATER

The ascended masters teach that the awakening and raising of the kundalini is intended to be a natural process—something that will happen gently and gradually as people evolve spiritually. When it is allowed to run its natural course, a beautiful blossoming of self-transcendence occurs. Higher powers may develop spontaneously when the student has purified his consciousness to the point that there is little danger of misusing these newly acquired powers.

Tips for Raising the Mother Light

There are several ways to facilitate the natural rising of the Mother light from the base-of-the-spine chakra to the crown chakra.

1. **Invoke the violet flame.** The consistent use of the violet flame will help to cleanse the aura, chakras and four lower bodies so they become pure energy conduits for the rising light. The action of the violet flame applies a gentle pressure that moves into the four lower bodies and dissolves impure residues in the chakras. As the misuses of light in our chakras are transmuted by the violet flame, the life force begins to rise in the same way that sap rises in a tree.

2. **Protect the light in your temple.** As individuals evolve spiritually, they increase the amount of spiritual light stored in their chakras and aura. It is important to protect that light from being channeled into wrong

7. Leadbeater, *The Chakras*, p. 83.

activities that lower its vibration, such as uncontrolled outbursts of anger. In the "Liberating Power of the Word" section in this chapter, you'll learn a short decree to invoke a cylinder of white light from your I AM Presence around you. This tube of light helps to seal your aura and chakras. And in chapters 6 and 7, you'll learn how to invoke the presence of Archangel Michael, who is the protector par excellence of your energy forcefield and your light.

3. **Give adoration to the Mother flame.** As stated earlier, the Mother light is anchored in the base-of-the-spine chakra and in the base of the threefold flame in the secret chamber of the heart. It's also found in nature and in the consciousness of the Divine Mother that permeates the universe. A simple and beautiful way to give adoration to the Mother flame within all of life is to give the Hail Mary prayer. Mary stands for Ma-ray—the Mother ray. In 1972, the Ascended Lady Master Mother Mary dictated to Elizabeth Clare Prophet a new version of the Hail Mary prayer, a traditional Catholic entreaty. The new version addresses the universal Ma-ray, personified in Mother Mary, and invokes her assistance as we evolve toward bonding with our own Christ consciousness as mature sons and daughters of God.

Giving this prayer with deep devotion gently raises up the Mother light from the base-of-the-spine chakra to the crown. You can enhance the raising of the energy by making gentle upward hand motions. With your hands cupped at your sides, raise them slowly from the level of the base-of-the-spine chakra to the level of your head. Repeat this motion while giving the prayer three times with deep devotion.

www.SummitLighthouse.org/SA1-9

Hail, Mary, full of grace,
The Lord is with thee.
Blessed art thou among women
And blessed is the fruit of thy womb,
Jesus.

Holy Mary, Mother of God,
Pray for us, sons and daughters of God,
Now and at the hour of our victory
Over sin, disease and death.

The Tube of Light

The effectiveness of decrees can be heightened by using certain time-proven techniques. Enunciating clearly, using proper rhythm and visualization, and repeating the words can increase the success of the science of the spoken Word. To practice these tips immediately, take the opportunity presented in this section to invoke the tube of light, that waterfall of spiritual energy that cascades down from your Higher Self to protect you twenty-four hours a day.

Pronunciation Makes a Difference

Decrees were dictated by the ascended masters, and their words are cups of light created in exact mathematical formulas that deliver spiritual light-energy into any situation. It is therefore important to articulate them clearly and precisely. This can be learned most easily by decreeing at a slow pace. Pronouncing the words at a relaxed speed also gives one a chance to focus on the meaning of the words. Contemplating the beautiful ideas embodied in each phrase helps the intent of the decree to manifest more fully and quickly, and so is a worthy endeavor for all students of the spoken Word.

It may take some effort at first to clearly pronounce the words of decrees because all of the muscles around the mouth must be active in order to move the lips, tongue and mouth. In decreeing, the best practice is to forget what you look like. An actively moving mouth may be an unusual sight, but the most effective decreers use a great deal of mouth movement. If you feel that your jaws are too tight to permit correct pronunciation, some jaw-stretching exercises can loosen them up and give your mouth the flexibility it needs to enunciate correctly.

Rhythm Sends Out Waves of Light

Establishing proper rhythm is another key aspect of giving decrees. Each decree has a definite sound pattern and pace. The rhythm is related to the specific action of the light released, so it is best to give decrees slowly until their cadences come naturally. One can then accelerate the pace of the decree.

Using correct rhythm permits a host of penetrating spiritual vibrations to project across the planet. These vibrations magnetize the qualities of God that are being invoked through the decree. They form great invisible waves carrying a certain momentum of light-energy. These waves are like rings that spread over the face of the earth to intensify the action of the invoked light everywhere they touch.

Great power is released when many people combine their energies and voices in a dynamic delivery. For instance, the Bible records that the walls of the city of Jericho were destroyed with a great shout. Prior to this shout, seven priests blew seven trumpets as the Israelites circled the city over the course of six days. On the seventh day, they circled Jericho seven times. During the seventh circling, the leader, Joshua, said to the people: "Shout, for the LORD hath given you the city...." The story continues: "So the people shouted when the priests blew with the trumpets. And it came to pass, when the people heard the sound of the trumpet and the people shouted with a great shout, that the wall fell down flat so that the people went up into the city, every man straight before him, and they took the city."[8]

You may have heard stories about armies marching over bridges causing the bridges to collapse. Just as the rhythm of an army marching in step can collapse a bridge, so the rhythm of a decree can create a strong spiritual force that breaks down accumulations of negative energy, habit patterns and undesirable karma. To learn the proper rhythm and speed with which to decree, practice decreeing with the online audio tracks.

Repetition Multiplies the Action

Repeating decrees multiple times gives greater benefit than giving them just once. In the East, people repeat mantras over and over, even thousands of times a day. But in the West, we are less accustomed to the idea of repeating a spoken request.

People often say, "Why should I have to ask God for something more than once?" But repeating a decree does not just reiterate a request to the heavenly hosts, it strengthens the waves of energy of the decree, which produces more profound results.

Every moment of each day, divine energy flows to us from our Higher Self. When we give mantras and decrees, we are charging this pure light, or "qualifying" it, in specific, constructive ways. The more we decree, the more positive energy we acquire and are able to send out into the world to bless others.

Imagine the process this way. You are sitting next to a stream and you pour a gallon of purple dye into it. The water in front of you turns a deep purple, but the purple water flows downstream and soon the water in front of you is clear

8. Joshua 6:16, 20, 21.

again. If you want to color the entire stream purple, you have to keep pouring gallons of purple dye into it.

It's the same way with any form of the spoken Word. Decreeing aloud for just a few minutes will affect a situation. But a serious circumstance may need ongoing attention. Saying a mantra or decree once is not always enough to overcome major problems. Repeating the decree reinforces the invoked action by multiplying its strength. As one repeatedly calls forth divine support from God, the energy builds and gains greater and greater power to produce constructive change.

The ascended masters teach that the angels need the momentum of our energy and our calls through decrees here below to do their work. Repeating decrees is one way we can invoke their reinforcing presence into stubborn and difficult conditions. When the ascended masters receive a decree message to take dominion over the sale of illegal drugs, for example, they send legions of angelic hosts, millions of angels, to do the job. A problem as large as the international drug trade involves billions of dollars and probably hundreds of thousands of people. In order to solve that problem, the angelic hosts have to intercede in a big way. Their armies of light and the hosts of heaven respond in huge numbers when a decree is repeated many times.

It is always best to repeat a decree at least three times whenever possible, amplifying it by the full power of your threefold flame. Later you can begin to increase your repetitions. Repeating the decree in multiples of three (6, 9, 12, 18, etc.) draws down the power of your I AM Presence and Holy Christ Self to produce even greater results. Repeating a decree 36, 48, 108 or even 144 times can access still more of the creative power of sound and accomplish astounding feats of good across the planet.

Putting on Your Tube of Light

In the Chart of Your Divine Self, you can see a large tube of light that looks like a white cylinder descending from the I AM Presence and surrounding the images of the Christ Self and the soul. In response to your spoken request, your I AM Presence is able to project its own light rays around your physical form so that you are surrounded by this beautiful tube of light, which is approximately nine feet in diameter. The tube of light tumbles down from ascended-master octaves like a waterfall of milky white substance. It surrounds your physical form and is invisible to the average person. This insulating tube can produce a forcefield of tremendous spiritual and physical protection.

In fact, your tube of light is the most important shield you have. It acts as a spiritual barrier against unwanted thoughts and feelings from other people, and it can also protect you from physical harm. Take the following story of Kobina, for example.

> Every day Kobina stood before the altar in his home and called forth his tube of light. While looking at the Chart of the Divine Self, he visualized his tube of light descending around him from his I AM Presence. He could feel the spiritual protection it gave him. But he also had firsthand experience of the very physical nature of its protection.
>
> Kobina was a high-ranking minister in the government of Kwame Nkrumah, president of Ghana, in western Africa. In 1966, a group of army officers initiated a bloody coup. Soldiers filled the neighborhood around the president's fortresslike residence and began firing into houses.

> Kobina's first concern was for his family, who lived near Nkrumah. He went home, piled them into the car and drove them away from the house. The soldiers noticed them and began shooting at the car, but they got away unharmed. In fact, Kobina recalls, "no bullet touched the car or any of us." At least twenty people were killed and over forty were wounded in and around the president's house that day, but Kobina and his family escaped. Was this just a fluke?
>
> Later Kobina had further proof of the protection of the tube of light. After he drove his family to safety, he went back home to get some of his belongings. The soldiers who had been arresting and shooting Nkrumah loyalists arrested him and talked about killing him. Somehow they didn't, but they sent him to a barracks where some other politicians had been taken. He was later exonerated by the new government.
>
> When he was allowed to go back home, escorted by soldiers, he discovered that the entire house had been looted, right down to the lightbulbs. But there was one thing the looters had not taken—the Chart of the Divine Self. He remembers that the soldiers told him that the looters had tried to take it. But "each time they attempted, they had an electric shock, as of fire; so they left it." This story traveled far and wide, leading many people in Ghana to a great respect for the I AM Presence.[9]

9. Elizabeth Clare Prophet, *Access the Power of Your Higher Self* (Gardiner, Mont.: Summit University Press, 1997), pp. 50–52.

SPOKEN WORD PRACTICE: "TUBE OF LIGHT" DECREE

The following exercise leads you through the process of putting on your tube of light. This wonderful spiritual armor is invoked through a decree called the "Tube of Light," which is usually given three times. Go to the online audio track to give the "Tube of Light" decree with Elizabeth Clare Prophet.

www.SummitLighthouse.org/SA1-10

1. When calling forth the tube of light it is customary to stand in honor and gratitude for one's I AM Presence. Standing also allows the tube of light to descend around the physical body to seal the aura and chakras. You may wish to place the Chart of Your Divine Self at eye level as an aid to visualization.
2. Visualize the tube of light from your mighty I AM Presence over you, extending around you to a diameter of about nine feet.

TUBE OF LIGHT

Beloved I AM Presence bright,
Round me seal your tube of light
From ascended master flame
Called forth now in God's own name.
Let it keep my temple free
From all discord sent to me.

I AM calling forth violet fire
To blaze and transmute all desire,
Keeping on in freedom's name
Till I AM one with the violet flame.

Chart of Your Divine Self

The "Tube of Light" decree can be given every morning after you wake up to create a shield of protection around you throughout the day. The "Tube of Light," as well as all other decrees, can last up to twenty-four hours. After that time, you must renew its action by invoking it again. You can even give it during the day for extra protection or just to feel secure in the arms of your mighty I AM Presence.

CHAPTER 5

Karma: Good, Bad and Balanced

How Free Will Shapes Your Life

Each of us holds the secrets to our own destiny. Free will is one of the most important keys we possess, and it stands among the greatest gifts we have received as co-creators with God. It allows us tremendous latitude for self-expression and creativity in pursuit of our divine ideals. In fact, our freewill use of light-energy is an integral part of our spiritual development and is directly related to karma, the law that states that we reap what we sow in life's endeavors. Understanding how this relationship works and considering the ways in which we make and balance karma can help accelerate our soul's expression of Spirit and hasten our reunion with our Higher Self.

Creating Ourselves by Qualifying Light

Chakras are major components of our spiritual identity. They function as distribution centers for the light-energy that constantly flows from the I AM Presence into our world. The process of distributing light through the chakras relates directly to another equally important process—qualifying that light. And how we qualify light is how we make karma, good or bad.

The life force that streams through our crystal cord comes to us as pure, crystal-clear energy. It descends over the cord as unqualified light carrying no particular characteristics or virtues. Since each chakra is governed by one of the seven spiritual rays, as the light from the I AM Presence flows through the different chakras, it is stamped with the specific vibration and color of the chakra and its corresponding spiritual ray.

Take the heart chakra as an example. As energy streams out through the heart chakra, it becomes qualified, or colored, with pink, the color of the third ray. The heart chakra is the place where we generate and experience the emotions of love and compassion. When this chakra is used correctly, the energy that flows through it takes on the vibrations of love. And when pure light-energy from the I AM Presence is properly qualified in the heart chakra, it flows out as pink light.

Heart Chakra

People continuously qualify divine light by their thoughts, feelings, words and actions. This process of qualifying, or coloring, the energy of Spirit happens automatically as the light flows through the chakras.

Free Will Choices

Our free will choices, expressed consciously or unconsciously, determine how the energy flowing through us is qualified and what kind of karma we are making. To understand the difference our free will choices can make, let's look at the heart chakra again. Say we make a conscious decision to send out love. When we feel love for our parents, children or friends, the energy flows through our heart chakra. Similarly, when we feel compassion for a hurricane or flood victim seen on television, our heart's energy reaches out to that person. The heart chakra is being used properly when the energy flowing through it is qualified with such positive feelings.

However, the heart chakra can also be used to qualify energy negatively. At times there may be a tinge of selfishness involved in feelings of love. Perhaps at some level the person sending love also desires something in return for that love. This element of self-centeredness causes a subtle change in vibration that affects the color of the light flowing through the heart chakra. In a less subtle example, irritation or dislike can flow from the heart towards another. And in extreme cases the heart can literally seethe with hatred. In these moments the light of the heart chakra is misqualified. When this occurs the vibration changes and the color manifests not as pure pink but as shades of orange, red or crimson that reflect dislike and hatred.

The energy that flows through each one of the chakras is similarly qualified by free will. Every chakra is simply an aperture for the flow of positively or negatively qualified light that is sent out into the world. The Eastern term that sums up the ramifications of this flow of energy is *karma*. Simply put, the vibration of the energy sent out results in karma—good and bad.

Karma: A Law of Life

The word *karma* shows up more and more regularly in the mass media. Although karma is fast becoming a household word, its meaning is not always clearly understood. People often interpret it as referring to one's luck or a randomly assigned fate or destiny. However, karma is far from a random event. In fact, it is a very precise law of life, and a thorough understanding of how it operates is important for anyone pursuing a spiritual path.

So what does karma mean? *Karma* is a Sanskrit word that means "action" or "deed," which also includes every thought, feeling and every spoken word. Both Hinduism and Buddhism teach that the law of karma is a universal law of cause and effect that applies to everyone.

The word *karma* may have an Eastern origin, but its general meaning is not new to the Western mind. The man on the street shows his understanding of karma when he says: "What goes around comes around." The Bible states the same concept: "Whatsoever a man soweth, that shall he also reap."[1] The law of karma

1. Galatians 6:7.

operates in the world and in everyone's life automatically and without partiality —recognized or not, believed or not.

Karma, as it appears in our lives, is the accumulated effect of all energy that we have ever sent out, knowingly or unknowingly. Our free will choices have qualified the light and energy properly or improperly. Every choice has certain effects and these effects can be observed and classified as good (positive) or bad (negative) karma.

Karmic Ties between Individuals

Karma is usually made with other people—those with whom we exchange energy or who are on the receiving end of the energy we send out. But although the bulk of people's karmic load is usually with other people, it's also possible to make karma with animals or other parts of life, such as an organization.

When karma is made between two people, it creates a tie between them, for better or for worse. This karmic tie is a bond that can keep bringing them together again and again. If the energy exchange is positive, it may result in a beautiful friendship that endures for a lifetime or beyond. If the karma is negative, it may lead to a difficult relationship that takes time and effort to resolve. Each of us has probably experienced a difficult person in our lives that we seem to keep "bumping into." That's because negative karma tends to keep bringing people into contact with each other until they learn the lesson that their relationship needs to teach them.

Karma permeates every aspect of life and all interactions. Yet not everything a person experiences is directly related to his own past actions or the past actions of others toward him. Since people have free will, anyone can make new karma at any moment. For example, someone may drive while they are drunk and injure another with whom he has no previous karma whatsoever. However, as soon as such new karma has been created, it becomes a part of the fabric of the lives of the two people involved.

Group Karma

In addition to individual karma, there's also "group karma." Group karma occurs when entire families, towns or nations have made karma with each other. Again this karma can be good or bad. Examples of negative group karma can be found among ethnic or religious groups whose hostilities stretch out over centuries, such as in Northern Ireland, the Middle East, the Balkans, or in the ongoing warfare between different African tribes. Not only do such actions create strong karmic ties between people, they also make individuals vulnerable to the effects of group karma. Natural disasters such as droughts, famines, earthquakes and floods are examples of ways in which group karma can return to entire communities or nations—the consequences of deeds committed or consented to as a group.

The Law of the Circle and the Law of Multiplication

Two more concepts add to a fuller understanding of how karma works. The first concept is that of the law of the circle, also known as the law of cycles. This spiritual law says that the energy that is released by God and man always returns to its point of origin. The second concept is the law of multiplication, which is based on the spiritual principle that "like attracts like."

Karma follows these spiritual laws. It brings back to your doorstep whatever energy you have sent out into the world. And it brings it back multiplied or intensified because it gathers more of the same kind of energy as it travels around on its way back to you. Let's consider these two laws from the perspective of the previous example of qualifying energy through the heart chakra.

Imagine yourself in the following situation. Your eight-year-old daughter comes home from school where she has just learned a new song. She can't wait to sing it to you. It's a joyous little tune and you smile as she sings. While she's performing for you, you feel your love for this precious child reaching out to her. And when she's done, you respond with glowing praise and a big hug. All through this interchange, a beautiful pink love-energy is flowing from your heart chakra to enfold your child. She feels loved and valued and radiates love back to you through her wonderful smile that warms your heart and fills you with joy. A brief exchange of energy just took place that uplifted both of you.

This simple event can be translated into karmic terms related to the law of the circle and the law of multiplication: you qualified the energy of your heart chakra positively, and in return you received a marvelous uplifting energy from your child, multiplied by the love of her heart.

Karma—to What End?

Karma is a law of life and it follows certain spiritual laws. But where does all this lead? What purpose does it serve? Above all else, karma is a teacher. It teaches the right and wrong use of energy, mostly through trial and error. Think of the energy sent out into the world as a kind of investment. We daily receive a certain portion of light from our I AM Presence and determine to invest it in certain energy patterns by means of our thoughts, desires, words and deeds. As the energy flows forth from us, it has an influence on the world around us. As it eventually returns to us multiplied, we receive our original "investment" with interest and can judge from the effects whether our investment was wise or not. As we learn the lessons that karma has to teach, we grow in wisdom, understanding, compassion and love. Indeed, we grow in divine consciousness and relate more and more to life from that perspective.

The Length of Karmic Cycles

Karmic cycles can be short, as in the previous example of the parent and child. Or they can be longer, because the energy that was released has its own way of cycling forth into the world. For instance, the child whom you loved may feel so great that when her big brother comes home from school, she greets him with intense joy and warmth. This, in return, may make him feel so good about himself that when he meets his friend that evening, the joy carries over and they have a wonderful time together, and so the cycle continues. Of course, at each of these contact points, a choice must be made in how the energy is perpetuated, but somehow it will keep cycling through the world. And it may take awhile before the full effect of what we have sent out returns to us. This example illustrates not only the length of karmic cycles but also the previously discussed law of multiplication.

So karmic cycles can last minutes, days, months, years or even longer. The cycle of returning karma may be so long that there is no way for us to know or recognize its origin. Good karma, such as rewarding relationships, might then be interpreted as "good luck." Bad karma, such as illnesses or other painful experiences, may cause the "Why me?" reaction, even though free will originally set these energies in motion and the consequences are only now returning.

In some cases, karmic cycles may be so long that they stretch out over lifetimes, where individuals reap their present karmic situation from past lives. This leads to the fascinating subject of reincarnation, which will be covered in detail in the next chapter.

Storing Our Treasures in Heaven

Even when karmic energy returns and is experienced fully, the cycle of energy is not yet concluded. Since the energy originated in the I AM Presence and not in the chakras, there is one last leg of its cyclic journey to be completed. The final step comes when it ultimately rises back to the level of the I AM Presence as beautifully qualified light-energy that is stored in the causal body.

This is the culmination of the intricate process by which we create our reality through our free-will use of energy. What was sent out from our I AM Presence as unqualified spiritual light has now been qualified with our unique vibration and the frequencies of the chakras through which we have released it. For instance, some of the earlier examples of how we qualify light illustrated how the light released through the heart chakra was stamped with the vibration of love, corresponding to the color pink. That energy, uniquely colored by us and received back as love and compassion, is deposited in the pink sphere of our causal body.

Causal Body

Proper use of light through each of the other chakras similarly increases other spheres of the causal body. Energy qualified with the frequencies of purity and harmony through the base-of-the-spine chakra rises into the white sphere. Energy that is qualified with wisdom and enlightenment through the crown chakra is deposited in the yellow sphere. The violet band is the repository for energy stamped with the vibrations of freedom and mercy through the seat-of-the-soul chakra. The energy colored with the frequencies of peace and brotherhood through the solar-plexus chakra is stored in the purple band of the causal body. The green band holds the pure energies of vision, truth and wholeness that come through the third eye. And the blue sphere receives the throat chakra's energy that is sent out as divine will, faith, power and determination.

Ultimately it is the preponderance of our unique preferences and accomplishments that gives individual identity to our causal body. For example, if a person always had a strong inclination towards science or the healing arts and has spent considerable time perfecting her talents in those areas, her causal body will have a strongly developed green band with many shades and nuances of emerald green light. Someone who has frequently been in leadership roles might have a powerful blue sphere dominating the others. And a person who has spent much time in contemplation and meditation will manifest strong yellow qualities in his causal body.

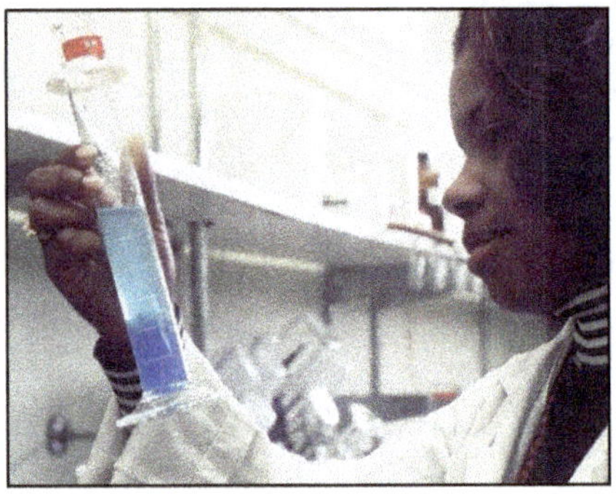

The light energy generated by giving decrees and affirmations also ascends to the causal body and increases the sphere of the ray that the decree invokes. At the same time, these decrees purify the energy in the individual's chakras and aura, and create a positive influence in his life and in the lives of those around him.

The bands of our causal body are the treasures of our good works stored in heaven. They contain the energy of all that is of value and nobility that we have ever created throughout our existence. The light-energy of our accumulated talents and accomplishments are available from our Higher Self, and we can draw on them throughout our life. For instance, perhaps as a child you excelled in drawing or painting but once you got into a busy career you lost interest. If you now want to continue developing your artistic side, you can call to your mighty I AM Presence to release to you the artistic skills and talents you developed previously in this life, or in all of your past embodiments.

This tapping into the riches of our causal body is only the beginning. As we balance more and more karma, more and more light of the causal body is actually anchored in the aura to uplift ourselves and others. Full access to this treasure trove of accomplishments is gained through reunion with the I AM Presence in the ritual of the ascension. In fact, the causal body then becomes our unique ascended master light body—unique because no one else has had the same experiences and victories. This is the glorious promise that our causal body holds for us!

Now you have a general understanding of how we use free will, make karma and participate in creating the circumstances of our lives. Gradual reunion with the Christ Self and then the I AM Presence is the ultimate goal of our journey. During this process, what began as an indistinguishable drop in the ocean of divine consciousness becomes a fully individualized spiritual being—a soul with unique talents and attainment. We each play a role in cosmic evolution that no one else can play and complete a mission that no one else can fulfill. This mission is the very purpose of our existence, and it's ours to discover in the midst of life—the sacred adventure.

Lay not up for yourselves treasures upon earth, where moth and rust doth corrupt and where thieves break through and steal. But lay up for yourselves treasures in heaven, where neither moth nor rust doth corrupt and where thieves do not break through nor steal. For where your treasure is, there will your heart be also.[2]

—JESUS CHRIST

MEDITATION: DRAWING DOWN THE LIGHT OF YOUR CAUSAL BODY

This meditation presents a method to magnetize the light of your causal body to fill your aura. It is derived from a dictation given by the Ascended Master Gautama Buddha through the messenger Elizabeth Clare Prophet on July 4, 1992. In this dictation, Gautama said:

> Let us understand and receive the meditation of the rings of the causal body, the mighty spheres of light. O most beloved ones, if you should one day enter into the congruency of the great Dharmakaya,[3] into the heart of hearts of the I AM THAT I AM, you will then be in the presence of and come to know those great and mighty spheres of the causal body of God.
>
> Now then, by way of magnetizing below that which is above, let us begin to realize and to visualize these rings. See them as flat rings that are horizontal. Then visualize them extending from your heart chakra, one upon the other, as you look at the great causal body on the Chart of the Presence. . . .
>
> See these rings as extending, beloved. See them going out. See the fiery power of the white, the yellow, the pink, the violet, the purple, the green and the blue. See that mighty action, beloved ones, and know that each day as you fill in those rings by action, by prayer, by determination, by will, by all that you do to the glory of God, as Above, so below, you are becoming that auric emanation of your God. . . .[4]

---

2. Matthew 6:19–21.
3. *Dharmakaya* (Sanskrit): the Body of Essence, the Body of the Law or Truth. The third body of the *trikaya* (the three bodies of the Buddha); the 'essence-being' of all Buddhas, immutable and undifferentiated, identical with absolute knowledge or Reality. This body equates with the I AM Presence and causal body.
4. *Pearls of Wisdom,* vol. 35, no. 41, p. 516.

Meditation Steps

1. Center in your heart and chant the *Aum* to establish peace in your four lower bodies.

2. Look at the picture of the causal body. Observe the color bands and note the sequence of the colors of the different bands extending outward from the center: white—yellow—pink—violet—purple—green—blue. Continue to gaze at the causal body until you can see the bands in your mind's eye.

Causal Body

3. Visualize your heart chakra as a blazing white-fire sun in the center of your chest.

4. See the rings of the causal body extending horizontally from your heart, starting with white in the center and ending with blue on the periphery. Visualize all of the rings until they are visible to your inner eye. If you forget which color comes next at any time, open your eyes and look at the picture of the causal body.

5. Try to feel the great power of these rings as they pulsate and radiate their light through your aura. Feel your aura and entire body being bathed in the light of the seven rays.

6. Sustain this visualization for as long as you are comfortable.

7. Send feelings of gratitude to your mighty I AM Presence for all of the light and beauty that is stored in your causal body.

8. Conclude your meditation by chanting the *Aum*.

9. Record your experiences in your journal.

Lessons in Earth's Schoolroom

Not all of the energy that we have sent out through our chakras makes it back to the causal body. What happens to the energy that was stamped with patterns of imperfection or impurity? What about the hurts, dislikes, arrogant behaviors, worries, resentments and fears that have flowed from our chakras out into the world?

This negatively qualified energy naturally returns to us as "bad" karma. The energy is not able to rise to the causal body, since it has a certain density that is incompatible with the high frequency of light-energy in the causal body. Until it is changed back into pure, positive energy it remains in the forcefield of our four lower bodies. It clogs up the chakras and prevents them from spinning and radiating at full capacity, which in turn reduces the flow of energy available for our use. This negative energy permeates the aura, where it manifests as jagged patterns and muddy colors that do not reflect the pure vibrations of the seven rays. Eventually, it collects in the lower half of the aura as karmic records and discordant energy patterns.

The ascended masters use the term *electronic belt* to refer to the lower half of the aura where these records accumulate. This is the portion of our spiritual anatomy that we might call the "ugly" part, as opposed to the beautiful light of our causal body. Our subconscious and unconscious records can be found here as components of our negative karma, built up over all our embodiments. This collected negative energy doesn't just sit within the aura and consciousness. It can weigh us down, so to speak, since it is directly related to psychological and emotional imbalance. It is ultimately responsible for physical problems, disease, old age and death. It's the opposite of the buoyant energy in our causal body that is magnetizing us to spiritual realms.

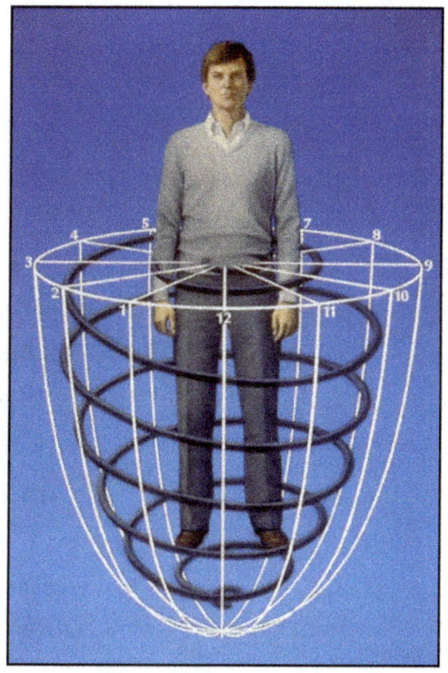

The Electronic Belt

So the slowing down and densification of the chakras and four lower bodies is the price we pay for energy unwisely invested. This is not punishment, but a karmic lesson that teaches us to make better choices and decisions regarding our use of the divine energy entrusted to our care. In fact, negative karma may serve as the best teacher in this world—if the recipient is willing to listen and embrace it as a mirror and an instructor of his soul.

Balancing Karma

In surveying the karmic scene with its beauty and its challenges, it is important to realize that karma and energy patterns are not set in stone. Energy is always in motion. It can be changed in polarity, from negative to positive, and it can be raised in vibration by a conscious effort. Therefore, any negative karma that may have been incurred in this and previous lifetimes can be exonerated or "balanced."

Making negative karma can be compared to borrowing money from a bank and then making a bad investment. The burden of this financial mistake doesn't go away until the debt is fully balanced. The ongoing balancing of negative karma is just as much a part of walking a spiritual path as is the acceleration of consciousness. In fact, it is necessary to balance negative karma in order to become truly free and reunite with the I AM Presence.

Ways to Balance Karma

Balancing karma is not just a cut and dried process—it involves many dynamics of energy flow. Say John injured Jane. Does that mean that Jane must injure John to balance the karma—or does it mean that someone else injuring John could balance it? Can the karma be balanced in some impersonal way? Is there less karma if the injury was an accident than if it were premeditated and done with malice? These questions could go on and on. It's easy to see that many elements of energy flow can be involved in the balancing of a particular karma. The next chapter covers more of these dynamics. Basically, the ascended masters teach that there are three different ways to balance negative karma: by enduring it, by serving life and by transmuting it.

Enduring Karma

Enduring karma means letting the negative energy come back and living through it with some grace. This is the most passive form of karma-balancing and takes place naturally over the course of time. Most people in the world are simply at the receiving end of their karma. As it returns to them, they let it work itself out as they suffer or struggle through it in the normal experience of their daily life. For example, negative karma can manifest in one's body as fatigue, illness or a handicap. It can crop up as friction, antagonism and other challenges in relationships. It can take the shape of the myriad circumstances and events in a life, perhaps manifesting as misfortune or a sudden accident. It can disguise itself as natural disasters that affect some yet allow others to escape miraculously.

By remaining calm and unattached in the midst of these challenges and viewing them as lessons that can help us to reevaluate our lives, we allow our returning karma to work itself out. On the other hand, becoming angry or upset about one's lot in life can create new karma in the old pattern, reinforcing the original karma and causing it to keep returning until finally the soul understands the deeper meaning of the experience and changes her ways.

Serving Life

Service to life is a more dynamic method of karma-balancing. Life can be served through family relationships, jobs and in harmonious interactions. In fact, we can view everyone who comes into our life as an opportunity to balance karma —from the stranger we meet on the bus to our grocery store clerk to the surgeon performing our operation.

It is also good to look for ways to serve life that will earn additional good karma to offset negative karma. We can reach out to others and go the extra mile with them. Or we could care for a chronically ill friend, volunteer as a fire fighter or a hospice worker, mow an elderly neighbor's lawn, spend Saturdays working at a shelter for the homeless, clean up littered highways or plant trees in deforested areas. There are myriad examples of ways we can earn good karma in service to the life that surrounds us. And the masters say that this good karma of serving helps to balance any negative karma we may have made.

Transmuting Karma with the Violet Flame

Using the high-frequency energy of the violet flame is a revolutionary spiritual method that helps to quickly balance negative karma. The violet flame has the power to transmute karma and restore misqualified energy to its original pure state. It is the most effective spiritual means of tackling the cause, effect, record and memory of negative karma. Those who have used the violet flame consistently testify that it clearly lightens their karmic load and is an amazing adjunct to their spiritual path.

Karma Can Be Mitigated

The violet flame may not be able to relieve *all* karma, because some of it may need to be experienced for the sake of learning lessons and growing spiritually. So even with the diligent use of the violet flame, bigger or smaller chunks of returning negative karma may need to be experienced. The hopeful news is that this may take the form of what is called mitigated or "token" karma. Mitigation occurs when the full impact of karma can be lessened because of merit gained through service to life, dedication to a spiritual path or grace that is extended to the soul. So one may receive token karma to balance what would otherwise have been a more severe negative return.

A STORY OF TOKEN KARMA

In his book Autobiography of a Yogi, *Paramahansa Yogananda gives a striking example of token karma—in this case, administered by an enlightened teacher who could read his student's karmic records. The setting is a group of disciples sitting around a huge fire with their guru, the great master Babaji. At some point, Babaji suddenly seized a burning brand from the fire and lightly struck one of his disciples on the shoulder.*

One of his chief disciples, Lahiri Mahasaya, protested this deed, "Sir, how cruel!" Babaji replied, "Would you rather have seen him burned to ashes before your eyes, according to the decree of his past karma?" Babaji placed his healing hand over the burn on the disciple's shoulder and said to him: "I have freed you tonight from painful death. The karmic law has been satisfied through your slight suffering by fire."[5]

SELF-REFLECTION: FREE WILL AND KARMA

Take some time to consider the different aspects of qualifying light and making karma explained in this chapter, especially any new concepts. Use the following questions to guide your reflections. You may wish to write your responses in your journal.

1. In what ways do I see myself making good karma in my life? (You may wish to list specific incidents here.) What are the ways in which I positively qualify the light-energy of my chakras?
2. In what ways do I recognize that I make negative karma? (List specific incidents, if desired.) What are the ways in which I negatively qualify the light-energy flowing through my chakras?
3. If I could change one aspect of myself right now, what would it be? Why do I want to change it? How would I like to change it? What do I need to do to bring about this change?

5. Paramahansa Yogananda, *Autobiography of a Yogi,* 11th ed. (Los Angeles, Calif.: Self-Realization Fellowship, 1979), p. 349.

Increasing the Effectiveness of Your Decrees

We all want to get the most out of the time we spend doing anything. Spiritual practices are no different. We want them to work as quickly, as easily and as well as possible. The tips contained in this section are directed toward this end. You can enjoy your decrees more and enhance their power by giving them in an appropriate decree environment, maintaining proper posture and using correct breathing. You can also increase their impact by sounding the words with the authority of your Christ Self and centering in your heart while visualizing the intended outcome. Try these techniques to observe their effectiveness for yourself.

Choosing a Place to Decree

It is best to decree in a room where you will not be disturbed. It helps to keep the room clean, well lighted and well aired. Dust, clutter, stale air and poor lighting reduce the effectiveness of decrees because they impede the flow of light that you are calling forth. They can also repel the angels, who always help to amplify the energies released from your I AM Presence and the masters. You may also wish to have a desk or table and chair in the room to facilitate your decree work.

Your Decree Posture

Maintaining proper posture while you are decreeing will help the light you invoke to flow more freely through your spiritual centers. If you sit with your spine straight and hold your head erect, your seven major chakras are aligned. This helps the energy move more easily through the chakras into your four lower bodies. Some people find that a straight-backed chair is a great aid to proper posture. You may also sit in a full- or half-lotus position if that is more comfortable for you.

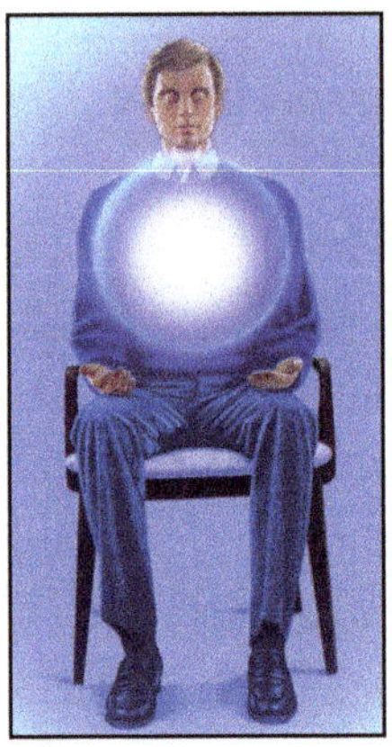

When sitting in a chair, it is best to have your arms and legs uncrossed and your feet flat on the floor. Crossing your legs and hands causes a "short circuiting" of the energies invoked. Having your feet touch the ground lets the light you are calling down course freely through you and be anchored in your environment. It is also helpful to have your hands cupped palms up in your lap. Since there is a secret-ray chakra in the center of each of your hands, holding your hands cupped when you decree allows these chakras to receive more of the light flowing to you from your Higher Self.

As you decree, you can help maintain a straight spine by holding the printed decree at or slightly below eye level. This keeps the neck from bending down to read the decree. You may want to sit at a desk or table where you can prop the decree page against a book or other object, thus leaving your hands free to receive the blessings you are invoking. Repetition facilitates memorizing the decree, allowing you to avoid this problem.

Breathing Deeply

Decreeing works best when you breathe deeply and regularly. A deep, powerful breath can project the light-energy through your chakras. One way to get into the habit of proper breathing is to practice the following technique. As you breathe in deeply, push your belly out. Then press your breath out by drawing your belly in. This action focuses your attention on your lower abdominal area and diaphragm, which helps your lungs to fill properly from the bottom. If you do this exercise often, you will find that breathing deeply will come much more easily. You can then decree with more power and greater effect.

When you are ready to begin a decree session, take a slow, deep breath. Blow all of the air out of your lungs, then breathe in slowly. You may wish to chant the Aum or I AM THAT I AM slowly in one or more out-breaths before you begin your session as an aid to attuning with your Higher Self.

As you decree, keep your breathing slow and rhythmic. Try not to let yourself get out of breath. Make an effort to slow down your breathing so that you can say the phrases smoothly and so that you can put maximum power into the words. In doing this, your lungs will cooperate with your brain and vocal cords to draw down the greatest amount of light from your I AM Presence.

Speaking with Authority

When you give an affirmation or decree, you give it by the authority of your Holy Christ Self and I AM Presence instead of your human consciousness. And when you are properly attuned, your Higher Self actually gives the decree and becomes its fulfillment on earth.

The physical sound and vibration involved in giving a decree is a part of the process of anchoring spiritual light in the physical plane. This process is enhanced when you can decree in full voice. The purpose of speaking robustly is to clearly and strongly direct the light of your mighty I AM Presence to positively change conditions for yourself, your family, your community and the world.

Speaking in a strong voice can usually release more power than speaking in a whisper. But speaking in full voice is not always possible. Typical examples of this would be decreeing in a public place or in an apartment building or in the same room with someone who's studying or sleeping. In such cases, it is obviously better to decree in a low voice or under your breath or even in your mind than to not decree at all. And even more important than decreeing in full voice is centering in the love of your heart when you give a decree.

Centering in the Love of Your Heart

Spiritually minded people everywhere regard the heart as a source of tremendous energy and power. We know that the heart is the place within where God resides, our point of contact with Spirit and our source of inspiration and self-transcendence. Connecting with the flame in the secret chamber of the heart is especially valuable when you practice the science of the spoken Word because it can greatly amplify the action of decrees.

The ascended masters have told us that the love in our hearts determines the power of our decrees. When we pour out our devotion and gratitude to God, we create a pathway to our Higher Self and the ascended masters that allows them to send a return current of that love to us. Sending love from your heart center while giving decrees can actually intensify their power as much as a thousandfold.

Centering in your heart may also enable you to draw down the light from your Higher Self in a powerfully open and intuitive way. Some people find that when they make contact with their heart flame they immediately feel a direct connection with their Christ Self and I AM Presence. This contact represents an inner attunement that produces greater sensitivity and focus when decreeing and allows more light to move into and through you.

Visualizing for Greater Results

Visualization is simply creating mental visual images. Some people can do this easily and even see things in their third-eye chakra as though they were seeing a photo or watching a TV screen. Most of us visualize by imagining in our mind. Either way works.

Visualization has been proven to enhance achievement in many areas of endeavor. To achieve greater success, sports enthusiasts, dramatists and lecturers visualize themselves victoriously practicing their craft before they perform. And succeed they do! In fact, university studies have proven that the human mind makes no distinction between mental visualization and actual physical activity.

We can capitalize on this by using visualization to increase the effectiveness of the science of the spoken Word. Consciously focusing on the image of what we want to create helps the I AM Presence to fulfill our commands. This is because visualization acts like a magnet to attract the creative energies of Spirit to fill the blueprint held in our mind.

Because visualization is such an important amplifier, it is good to use it each time you decree, if possible. Memorizing decrees will make this easier. Focus on visualizing the main positive outcome of your decree. For example, if you want to dissolve tension in a relationship, visualize the violet flame surrounding yourself and the other person as you give decrees to invoke the violet flame.

If you have difficulty visualizing, the decree will still work. But if you are able to visualize the desired action, you will find that the results are often achieved more easily and quickly. In the following exercise, "Expanding the Power of Your Decrees," you can practice visualizing the violet flame. You may wish to try this simple little assignment before you do that exercise if you think visualizing might be difficult for you.

1. Light a candle.
2. Focus on the flame for several seconds.
3. Close your eyes.
4. See the flame in your mind's eye.
5. Mentally color the flame violet.
6. Repeat steps 1–5 until you can form a clear image of a violet flame.

Putting It All Together

Using the science of the spoken Word allows energy to cycle through all of your four lower bodies to create a better life and a better world. You use the physical and emotional bodies to bring forth the Word. Your posture, breathing and throat chakra are used to invoke the energy the decree calls forth. Centering in your heart uses your etheric body as a pure and holy conduit for the light. And visualization uses your mental body to set the perfect pattern for the light to follow. So putting all of these things together allows for the greatest release of light from Spirit into matter and puts you in your rightful place as co-creator with God.

SPOKEN WORD PRACTICE: EXPANDING THE POWER OF YOUR DECREES

This exercise will give you the opportunity to practice all of the techniques discussed in this spoken Word section. Following these steps when you give any decree will help you to have a more effective session and can produce greater benefits. This practice includes a new decree to the violet flame, "Radiant Spiral Violet Flame."

1. Find a clean, well-lighted room where you will not be disturbed. Sit at a desk or table that will allow you to prop up the decree page at a level that is comfortable for your eyes without causing you to bend over.
2. Sit in a straight-backed chair with your arms and legs uncrossed, your feet flat on the floor and your hands cupped in your lap, or in a lotus/half-lotus position.
3. Close your eyes and take about 30 seconds to breathe deeply from your belly until you feel calm and centered. On the last breath out, chant I AM THAT I AM slowly and deliberately.

www.SummitLighthouse.org/SA1-11

4. Focus your attention on your heart, going deep within. Recall a favorite event or scene that brings about a feeling of love, gratitude or appreciation. Let these pleasant feelings expand and grow stronger.

5. Visualize violet flame filling your aura. You may wish to use an image of the violet flame as an aid to this visualization. See the violet flame extending in all directions around you to a diameter of about nine feet.

Soul in Physical Form

6. Give the following decree three times slowly and deliberately while holding the visualization of the violet flame.

RADIANT SPIRAL VIOLET FLAME

(Preamble)

In the name of the beloved mighty victorious Presence of God, I AM in me, and my very own beloved Holy Christ Self, I decree:

(Decree Body)

Radiant spiral violet flame
  Descend, now blaze through me!
Radiant spiral violet flame,
  Set free, set free, set free!
Radiant violet flame, O come,
  Expand and blaze thy light through me!
Radiant violet flame, O come,
  Reveal God's power for all to see!
Radiant violet flame, O come,
  Awake the earth and set it free!
Radiance of the violet flame,
  Expand and blaze through me!
Radiance of the violet flame,
  Expand for all to see!
Radiance of the violet flame,
  Establish mercy's outpost here!
Radiance of the violet flame,
  Come, transmute now all fear!

(Closing)

And in full faith I consciously accept this manifest, manifest, manifest! (3x) right here and now with full power, eternally sustained, all-powerfully active, ever expanding and world enfolding until all are wholly ascended in the light and free!

Beloved I AM! Beloved I AM! Beloved I AM!

CHAPTER 6

Reincarnation: Beyond the Veil of This Life

Keys to Your Past, Present and Future

Thus far we've learned about our Higher Self, our spiritual anatomy, our freewill use of energy, and how we create karma. These topics lead to the natural consideration of reincarnation as the process through which we balance our negative sowings and reunite with our I AM Presence. Although the Divine resides within each of us, we cannot embrace it all at once. Rather, we do so incrementally day by day, year after year, lifetime after lifetime.

Historical and cultural perspectives on reincarnation are sometimes an eye-opener to the Western mind. Yet even a cursory consideration of the various factors that can necessitate a soul's need to reembody can be quite enlightening. In this vein, some fascinating case studies and scientific findings illustrating reincarnation are included here. The perspectives of the Bible and the ascended masters are brought to light, as well. Reading with an open mind and heart will provide the greatest understanding of these various viewpoints.

> *My life as I lived it had often seemed to me like a story that has no beginning and no end. I had the feeling that I was a historical fragment, an excerpt for which the preceding and succeeding text was missing. I could well imagine that I might have lived in former centuries and there encountered questions I was not yet able to answer; that I had to be born again because I had not fulfilled the task that was given to me. When I die, my deeds will follow along with me—that is how I imagine it. I will bring with me what I have done. In the meantime it is important to insure that I do not stand at the end with empty hands.*[1]
>
> —CARL JUNG

Life Goes On

Like Carl Jung, the spiritual seeker hopes that at the end of his life he will not stand with "empty hands." Therefore, he takes care in writing the story of his life day by day. He carries out his various roles to the best of his ability. These roles may be parent, student, friend, spouse, employee or boss. And although doing

1. Carl Jung, *Memories, Dreams, Reflections,* quoted in Joseph Head and S. L. Cranston, comps. and eds., *Reincarnation: The Phoenix Fire Mystery* (New York: Crown Publishers, 1977), p. 560.

one's best takes a lot of effort, each soul knows that by continual striving she will eventually reach the goal of reuniting with her I AM Presence. In the context of striving to reach the goal of life, reincarnation figures as a solution to the challenge of balancing karma.

It is easy enough to make negative karma, but it is not always so easy to balance it. The law of karma is exact. Karma can be made with specific individuals and, in order to balance that particular karma, the soul may have to wait for all the souls originally involved to be present again or for the same situation to occur again, or both. She may even have to wait lifetimes.

According to the law of karma, the thoughts, words and deeds of past lives have determined the conditions of one's present life. And the thoughts, words and deeds in this life will determine one's destiny in future lives. Past lives and future lives? While some readers may already believe in reincarnation, it may be a new concept for others. The following reflections on reincarnation may help those who are less familiar with the concept to come to a deeper understanding.

Views from History

Reincarnation is regarded in many different ways across the planet. It is interesting to note how widely accepted it is in some arenas and how skeptically it is viewed in others. Let's look at the evidence history presents for reincarnation.

All the world's a stage,
And all the men and women merely players:
They have their exits and their entrances,
And one man in his time plays many parts.[2]

—SHAKESPEARE

Before the advent of Christianity, reincarnation was part of the spiritual beliefs of many of the peoples of Europe, including the early Teutonic tribes, the Finns, Icelanders, Lapps, Norwegians, Swedes, Danes, early Saxons, and the Celts of Ireland, Scotland, England, Brittany, Gaul and Wales. The Welsh have even claimed that it was the Celts who originally carried the belief in reincarnation to India. Author Ignatius Donnelly suggests that the Celts' belief in reincarnation was derived from the inhabitants of the lost continent of Atlantis who had migrated to Ireland.[3]

The belief in reincarnation has spanned all the continents and touched countless peoples. According to some scholars, statements made by the first-century Jewish historian Josephus indicate that the Pharisees and Essenes believed

2. Shakespeare, *As You Like It,* act 2, sc. 7, lines 138–41.
3. Ignatius Donnelly, *Atlantis: The Antediluvian World,* rev. ed., ed. Egergon Sykes (New York: Gramercy Publishing Company, 1949), pp. 251, 254–55.

in reincarnation. Some tribes of American Indians as well as numerous tribes in Central and South America believed in reincarnation. And reincarnation was taught by students of the Kabbalah, an ancient system of Jewish esoteric mysticism, whose teachings were first published in the thirteenth century. The belief in reincarnation is still held by those in the Jewish Hasidic movement, founded in the eighteenth century.

Today more than one hundred tribes in Africa believe in reincarnation. Others accepting this doctrine include Eskimo and Central Australian tribes and many peoples of the South Pacific, including Hawaiians, Tahitians, Melanesians and Okinawans. The most elaborately developed concepts of reincarnation today are found in the religious traditions of India, especially Hinduism, Buddhism, Jainism and Sikhism.

Famous people throughout history have believed in reincarnation, as well. These include Pythagoras, Plato, Origen of Alexandria, Nietzsche, Ralph Waldo Emerson, Kahlil Gibran, Benjamin Franklin, General George Patton and Henry Ford, to name a few.

So why are some people reluctant to accept this historically established doctrine? Most objections in the West have come from Christians who say that reincarnation is against the principles that Jesus taught. Though these individuals comprise a minority of the billions of people on the planet, they have been quite vocal and adamant. Their viewpoint is worthy of being addressed in order to help clear up confusion.

Jesus' Teachings on Reincarnation

The Christian argument against reincarnation is based chiefly on doctrine and dogma handed down for centuries that do not endorse it as a belief. Opponents say that reincarnation is not in the Bible and Jesus didn't teach it, therefore, it is not real or true. Yet scholars have studied the various translations of the Bible and found that the thousands of existing New Testament manuscripts and Bible quotes preserved in ancient writings differ from each other in over 250,000 ways. Various alterations have removed certain portions and even entire biblical books over the centuries, some intentionally and some unintentionally. Starting with the Council of Nicaea in A.D. 325 through the Fifth General Council of the Church in 553, clear teachings on reincarnation were removed from the Bible and therefore from the Christian faith.[4] However, some references still appear in the Bible favoring the supposition that Jesus believed in reincarnation.

The Man Born Blind

Consider this passage: "As Jesus passed by, he saw a man which was blind from his birth. And his disciples asked him, saying, 'Master, who did sin, this man or his parents, that he was born blind?' Jesus answered them, 'Neither hath this

4. *Pearls of Wisdom,* vol. 40, no. 23, p. 140.

man sinned nor his parents, but that the works of God should be made manifest in him.'"[5]

The question the disciples asked indicates that they had a deep understanding of spiritual law as well as the scripture of their day. They knew about the laws of karma and reincarnation since they knew that this man could have been born blind because of his sins. If he was born with sin, then surely he must have lived before. They also knew the Old Testament law in the Book of Numbers that says that the sins of the fathers shall be visited upon the children to the third and fourth generations.

According to the Gospel writer John, Jesus did not make an issue about reincarnation, even though this conversation of his disciples was based on knowledge of karma and reincarnation. He did not correct the disciples or rebuke them; he simply answered that it was neither of the situations they mentioned. The man hadn't sinned. His parents hadn't sinned. But he had come into embodiment born blind by his free will so that Jesus could heal him and that the works of God could be manifest in him and the glory of God could be revealed. This incident indicates that discussions on the doctrine of reincarnation may have occurred between Jesus and his disciples.

Elijah Come Again

Let's look at another teaching of Jesus involving reincarnation. Three of the disciples, Peter, James and John, were coming down the Mount of Transfiguration with Jesus. On the mountain, the disciples had seen Moses and Elias appear to Jesus and talk with him. *Elias* is the Greek name for the prophet Elijah, who lived in the ninth century B.C. The disciples asked Jesus, "Why then say the scribes that Elias must first come?" referring to the prophecy that Elias would come before the Messiah to prepare the way for him. In other words, they were asking why Elias was appearing to Jesus out of heaven instead of going before him as it was prophesied. Jesus replied: "'Elias truly shall first come and restore all things. But I say unto you, that Elias is come already, and they knew him not but have done unto him whatsoever they listed.

John the Baptist was a prophet who lived during the time of Jesus, baptizing the Jews and exhorting them to repent of their sins and prepare for the coming of the mighty one who would baptize them with the Holy Spirit. John had rebuked Herod, the king of Judea, for marrying his brother's wife, whereupon Herod imprisoned him and later had him beheaded. He lived nine hundred years after the prophet Elijah.

5. John 9:1–3.

Likewise shall also the Son of man suffer of them.' Then the disciples understood that he spake unto them of John the Baptist."[6]

They understood that Jesus was talking about John the Baptist because they already knew the doctrine of reincarnation. The very belief among the Jews of Jesus' day that the prophet Elijah would come again as the forerunner of the Messiah shows a belief in reincarnation. So when Jesus said, "He's already come...," he was simply saying that Elijah had already reincarnated as John the Baptist.

In summary, these two instances with Jesus are valuable because (1) they show that reincarnation was a familiar topic to the Jews of that time and (2) rather than take exception to it, Jesus supported it. And there are other biblical references to reincarnation. If you would like to explore this topic further, *Reincarnation: The Missing Link in Christianity* by Elizabeth Clare Prophet with Erin L. Prophet is very thorough and well-documented reading.

Taking Responsibility Is Hard but Rewarding

While some doubt the doctrines of karma and reincarnation for religious reasons, others remain skeptical or reluctant to believe it for reasons that are harder to articulate. Swami Prabhavananda and Christopher Isherwood talk about this reluctance in their book *How to Know God.*[7] They say that accepting these truths means being willing to look at our lives and take full responsibility for them. And it is sometimes difficult for us to accept direct responsibility for personal negativity. There is a human tendency to look at the imperfections in our actions or in ourselves and to place the blame elsewhere. It is easy to blame God, parents, the environment or the social structure for the problems we face. It is harder to believe in karma and reincarnation, which make us accountable for our past actions and for any current difficult circumstances.

Since blaming others is often done subconsciously, we sometimes have the inaccurate perception that we are not accountable. This attitude bypasses the fact that the universal law of free will gives us sole culpability for our actions, and that the natural rule of justice governs the return of our karma based on those actions. It also makes us miss out on the joy of personal adventure and opportunity whereby we can say, "I got here by my own efforts and I can get anywhere I want by my own efforts."

When we adopt an attitude of responsibility, our soul leaps for joy since she is taking a big step toward union with her Higher Self. This in turn leads to being willing to change wherever needed so that she can come into greater alignment with her divine blueprint. Though hardships may occur along the way, the soul can more easily endure them when she knows that taking personal accountability will ultimately lead to true happiness.

6. Matthew 17:11–13.
7. *How to Know God,* trans. by Swami Prabhavananda and Christopher Isherwood (Hollywood, California: Vedanta Press, 1987).

The Answer to Some Common Questions

Having examined some of the historical and psychological aspects of believing in reincarnation, let's consider it from another angle—how it shows up as part of daily life in subtle and not-so-subtle ways. Reincarnation provides the answer to many common questions, but it is not always recognized as the answer. Here are some reflections on a few of those questions.

Déjà Vu

Have you ever done something or gone somewhere that seemed familiar, as if you had already done it or been there before? Or have you ever met someone you felt as if you already knew? Almost everyone has had such experiences. They are commonly referred to as *déjà vu,* from the French, meaning "already seen." Some may shrug such things off, while others realize that karma and reincarnation may be the reason for the familiarity. That's because these people and places may have been part of one's actual experience in a past life. The soul recognizes them and is trying to tell the conscious mind that they are not new to her.

Here is a very good example of déjà vu. Opera singer Risë Stevens recounted what happened to her during a performance she gave in an ancient amphitheater in Athens. While she was singing Orpheo's aria of lamentation at the foot of the Acropolis, she "lost all touch with reality." She felt herself returning to ancient Greece and reliving a former life where she had acted on the very same stage. She later wrote about the experience, saying that she finished the aria "as in a trance." It took five minutes of thunderous applause to bring her back to the present.[8]

Seeming Injustices

Looking around at the world and its billions of people, the spiritual student may start to wonder about many things. His heart and soul say that God is loving and that the universe is full of light. Yet the intellect questions why some people are born with riches and good looks, while others are born with deformities and in the worst of circumstances. Why are some people brilliant and others mentally retarded? Why do some people die in their sleep, while others die in war?

There is no more logical explanation for such variances than karma and reincarnation. It makes sense out of all such questions. It eliminates the seeming contradictions between a loving God and negativity existing in the world. Through freewill choices, we have used the light of the universe and created the current circumstances of our lives. Differences in the present reflect past actions coming

8. Kyle Crichton, *Subway to the Met: Risë Stevens' Story* (Garden City, N.Y.: Doubleday & Company, 1959), pp. 237–38.

full circle through the cycles of karma and reincarnation. Though we cannot always see the reasons for discrepancies in the present, we can understand that there is no injustice when we know about the stretch of cycles and past karma that led up to them.

Child Prodigies

It is natural to ask where child prodigies get their amazing talent. Mozart, for instance, began composing minuets at age three and completed his first symphony at age five. Could his extraordinary talent have come from his parents, early training or environment?

Past-life attainment offers the best explanation for such child prodigies, whose outstanding talents don't seem to be explained in any other way. These children are unusual by virtue of their age, yet they show that we can each access our own talents from previous lives by drawing them down from our causal bodies where they are stored.

Past-Life Memories

Some people remember past lives. These individuals are variously treated—put on a pedestal by some, viewed as psychologically imbalanced or insane by others, and ignored out of fear by yet others. Yet it can be life-changing to look at a person's past-life memories. Here is such a case.

A three-year-old girl in India, named Shanti Devi, began talking about her husband and children from her past life. She told her new family her previous husband's name and where they had lived. She described the house they lived in and said she had died after giving birth to her second child.

A relative of her former husband was sent to investigate. Shanti had never seen this man, yet she recognized him right away. She threw her arms around him and then told him about her past life. It was exactly as he had witnessed it. Then her former husband and son came to see her unannounced and she recognized them both immediately.

Shanti then led a committee of investigators to her previous home. She used idioms of speech familiar in that town, though she had never been there before. She even told the observers where she had buried some money before her death! Investigators eventually proclaimed this to be an authentic case of reembodiment.[9]

Remembering Past Lives

It is easy to wonder why we all don't remember our past lives if reincarnation is true. Considering the example above can help us answer that question.

9. The case of Shanti Devi's reincarnation is referred to in many publications, among them Dr. Ian Stevenson's *Children Who Remember Previous Lives: A Question of Reincarnation* (Charlottesville: University Press of Virginia, 1987) and "The Evidence for Survival from Claimed Memories of Former Incarnations," Part 1, *The Journal of the American Society for Psychical Research* 54 (April 1960).

We can acknowledge Shanti's deep emotions in her encounters with loved ones from the past as a touching tribute to the soul's tie to others. But we can also imagine that the complexity of living two lives at once was difficult for her to bear—and she was just three years old. Envisioning her distress can help us understand why cosmic law, in its infinite mercy, veils the past from most of us. This mercy of forgetfulness allows us to live each episode of the present free from detailed memories of former lives that might confuse current issues or cloud our decisions.

A person's recollection of past embodiments is often determined by the needs of the individual soul, as will be discussed later in the chapter. Yet the truth remains that, remembered or not, the records of our past incarnations stay in the depths of our soul and influence our present choices, attitudes and personality.

Why We Reincarnate

What's the reason behind reincarnation? Let's use an analogy from the world of nature.

Our life cycles and growth cycles can be compared to those of a chambered nautilus. The chambered nautilus lives in a shell that he lines with beautiful mother-of-pearl. As he lives in one chamber he is preparing the next, instinctively knowing that he will outgrow the present one. He moves from chamber to chamber, and when he dies he leaves his shell and moves on by dissolving and becoming one with the sea.

People live in a similar way. Consider the four lower bodies as the shell of the soul's habitation that allows her to move in the sea of consciousness. She spends a lifetime in a physical "chamber," or body, which provides the opportunity for filling her being with the beautiful rainbow light of cosmic consciousness. When the soul has "outgrown" the opportunity provided in the chamber of that body, she moves into the next one. Ideally, in each successive lifetime she grows and increases in light and universal awareness until she no longer needs the shell of a body to house her. That is when the soul moves out into the cosmic sea and becomes one with the very essence of life.

Think about the body as a vehicle for the soul's expression. Vehicles wear out. If we have a car that wears out, we get a new one because we still need to get places. It works the same way with the physical body. When it wears out, the soul gets a new one to take her where she is going—all the way home to union with the I AM Presence. Reincarnation is really that simple. Time moves on; the body wears out before we have gotten where we're going. So we put on a new body, gain more spiritual light and eventually arrive back home.

Life cycles are ongoing. Our soul did not begin when we were born, nor will she end when we die. Ideally, she gains increments of light during each cycle of cumulative experience. Our soul needs a long enough time to garner sufficient energy and reach the level of spiritual maturity required to achieve union with the I AM Presence. A single lifetime is just not enough time.

In addition to needing time to reunite with his divine source, the seeker needs time to balance the negative karma he has made. So the law of karma is fulfilled through the law of reincarnation. Bear in mind that karma is not determinism—it determines the basic circumstances of one's rebirth: parents, health and all of life's opportunities. But it does not determine one's actions. In other words, it provides the situation but not the response to the situation. So there is a free-will choice when negative karma returns: to balance it and pay the debt, or not. Reincarnation gives the soul the opportunity to learn the lessons that returning karma, good and bad, is trying to teach with exacting discipline. If one makes the choice not to balance karma when the opportunity arises in a given lifetime, reincarnation provides another chance.

Reincarnation is also a cosmic system of mercy whose cycles provide the framework for the soul to reach spiritual maturity. It affords the soul time to move through the varied experiences of being male and female, rich and poor, different nationalities, and so forth. And it provides her with the opportunity to encounter the myriad circumstances that assist her in learning karmic lessons so that she can move onward.

> *"I have had a dream, a whole lifetime, two thousand years ago!... A lifetime—childhood, boyhood, manhood. ... I have lived through a whole life in that old world....*
>
> *"As it happened, death came early enough for me to die with a living love still in my heart."...*
>
> *"To live again," said Sunray very softly.*
>
> *"And love again," said Sarnac, patting her knee....*
>
> *"It was a life," said Sarnac, "and it was a dream, a dream within this life; and this life too is a dream. Dreams within dreams, dreams containing dreams, until we come at last, maybe, to the Dreamer of all dreams, the Being who is all beings. Nothing is too wonderful for life and nothing is too beautiful."*[10]
>
> —H. G. WELLS

Reincarnation allows one to capitalize on the previous harvest of talents and good works, as well. It lets the soul gradually absorb the divine consciousness until she becomes the fullness of her Christ Self and provides the time she needs to fulfill her mission. She has to do these things in order to prepare for her ascension, break the rounds of rebirth and live in realms of higher consciousness.

The Past Is Prologue

The soul has journeyed through many lifetimes. This very moment is the culmination of all previous lives. The essence of the soul, with all her gifts, talents and attributes, is the result of her sowings on her journey through her previous embodiments. So, while it isn't necessary to know specifics of past lives, sometimes the past peeks through to help one take the next step forward in soul evolution. This has happened to a growing number of people who have pursued various forms of therapy—they have remembered past embodiments. Such cases point out the fact

10. H. G. Wells, *The Dream,* quoted in Eva Martin, comp., *Reincarnation: The Ring of Return* (New Hyde Park, N.Y.: University Books, 1963), pp. 280–81.

that the past is prologue to the future. As the lessons of the past are learned, progress is made on the spiritual path.

Investigative Research

There has been extensive investigative research into reincarnation in the last few decades. Much of it has been conducted by psychologists and psychiatrists, including a number who have used hypnosis.[11] Many of these doctors did not start out intending to probe past lives. Rather, they were forced to deal with the issue of reincarnation because, as they explored their patients' current problems, they were led to their past lives to find the answers.

Dr. Alexander Cannon speaks eloquently about not wanting to deal with reincarnation in his book *The Power Within*: "For years the theory of reincarnation was a nightmare to me and I did my best to disprove it and even argued with my trance subjects to the effect that they were talking nonsense. Yet as the years went by one subject after another told me the same story in spite of different and varied conscious beliefs. Now well over a thousand cases have been so investigated and I have to admit that there is such a thing as reincarnation."[12]

Dr. Helen Wambach, author of *Life Before Life,* was a clinical psychologist and regression-therapy expert who pioneered past-life and prenatal research. She regressed hundreds of people during her career and said, "Ninety percent of the people who come to me definitely flash on images from a past life."[13] She conducted extensive studies to prove or disprove the theory of reincarnation. She came to *know,* rather than just believe, that the process of reincarnation is real. She said, "If you are sitting in a tent on the side of the road and 1,000 people walk past telling you they have crossed a bridge in Pennsylvania, you are convinced of the existence of that bridge in Pennsylvania."[14]

Approaching reincarnation from a different angle, Dr. Ian Stevenson, a psychiatrist and the world's foremost investigator of children's past-life memories, prefers not to use hypnosis. Instead he interviews children who have already had past-life memories and then tries to independently verify the details of their

11. The ascended masters strongly caution their students against using hypnosis or autohypnosis. While people are hypnotized, they effectively surrender their free will and are not under the direction and protection of the Holy Christ Self. Hypnosis also opens one's subconscious mind to outside influence beyond one's control, allowing the subconscious and unconscious habit patterns, desires, etc., of the hypnotist to be transferred to the person's subconscious—regardless of the good intentions of both people. Yet hypnosis has added valuable insights to past-life research, such as those referenced here. If you want to discover your own past lives, there's no need to force the issue. The masters teach that they will be revealed to you according to your soul's need to know and understand certain karmic records as you progress on the spiritual path.
12. Alexander Cannon, *The Power Within,* quoted in Christopher M. Bache, *Lifecycles: Reincarnation and the Web of Life* (New York: Paragon House, 1990), p. 45.
13. Helen Wambach, *Life Before Life* (New York: Bantam Books, 1979), back cover.
14. Joel L. Whitton and Joe Fisher, *Life Between Life* (New York: Warner Books, 1986), p. 68.

previous existence. He has meticulously documented 2,500 of these cases—an impressive feat!

Then there is Dr. Joel Whitton, a Toronto psychiatrist, who has broken new ground in past-life hypnotherapy. He delves into the experiences of his subjects not just in their previous lives but also between lifetimes on earth. He refers to this space of time between lives as the "interlife." Interestingly, their experiences reveal information that is very similar to what those who have had near-death experiences have recounted.

Dr. Whitton's book *Life Between Life,* written with co-author Joe Fisher, is replete with interesting stories. The following is a glimpse at just one of these stories. A subject had gone through a series of lifetimes where he killed anyone who treated him badly. In this lifetime, his father treated him brutally as a child. He grew to hate his father and, as a teenager, came close to killing him in a particular incident. However, he followed an inner voice telling him not to do it and, from that moment on, his life turned around. He later learned that in the interlife he had chosen the difficult circumstances of his life in order to finally get the victory over the karmic pattern of his past actions.[15]

Key Elements in Reincarnation

It is noteworthy that the information in *Life Between Life,* as well as in books by other doctors, verifies through the personal experiences of patients much of what the ascended masters have taught concerning reincarnation. The following is a list of some common elements gleaned from investigative research that substantiate what the masters have told us about the journey of our souls.

- Karma is a teacher whose lessons span many lifetimes.
- If we fail a test, that test is repeated lifetime after lifetime until we pass it and learn its lesson.
- The reason we leave the interlife and return to embodiment is that physical life offers the best opportunity to increase our soul's awareness.
- Talents are progressively developed in incarnation after incarnation.
- Two of the main lessons to learn in life are love and forgiveness.
- A life review at the end of each embodiment helps the soul see its shortcomings and victories.
- Two or more compassionate counselors, often a board of counselors, work with us between lifetimes.

15. Ibid., pp. 75–76.

- In consultation with these counselors, each soul decides what she needs to do in the coming life and establishes a life span. What the soul needs and what she wants are not always the same.
- We often choose very difficult circumstances in order to maximize our soul's growth in a given lifetime.
- The counselors make recommendations, but the final decision regarding the coming life circumstance is ours to make.
- Life plans can change based on freewill choices made during a given lifetime.

One of the key elements from this list that needs further elucidation is the work of the board of counselors, or judgment board, mentioned in these studies. The ascended masters call this group the Karmic Board.

The Karmic Board—Our Loving Advisers

The Karmic Board is a group of seven ascended masters and lady masters. Vairochana, a Buddha of great attainment who has never embodied on earth, is the eighth member of this board. They are also called the Lords of Karma. The title "Lords" refers to their vast realization of divine consciousness. They administer justice in this solar system and adjudicate karma, mercy and judgment on behalf of every soul.

Every soul meets with the Karmic Board before and after each incarnation on earth. The soul may meet with three, four or all eight members of the board, depending on the need. These masters work with the soul before each lifetime to help her wisely decide her assignment and the returning karma she will encounter. They help arrange a life plan that will allow the soul to make as much spiritual progress as possible in a given embodiment. Then at the conclusion of that life, the Lords of Karma compassionately assist the soul in reviewing her performance.

The following true story is just one example of how the Lords of Karma worked with a soul to help her decide how to resolve and balance specific karma.

Story of a Karmic Debt

A baby girl was born into a family of fishermen in Denmark in the ninth century. As she grew up, a young fisherman was attracted to her, but she wasn't really interested in him. He went out on a long fishing trip with his father and upon his return, he went to her house with lustful desires. She was preparing vegetables for dinner and had a carving knife in her hand. He made advances toward her. When she rebuffed him, he raped her. In her outrage against this violation, she killed him with the knife.

What follows is a description of the karmic consequences of the woman's actions, as revealed by Elizabeth Clare Prophet and the ascended masters. Of course, there were also karmic consequences for the man in this story. The details of his karma, however, have not been revealed to us.

At the conclusion of that embodiment, the woman went before the Lords of Karma and saw the murderous scene clearly. She knelt and sobbed and said: "I will do anything to balance this karma. I will serve this person as long as you will have me serve him. Let me give him back the life I took from him." And so the Lords of Karma assigned her to a number of embodiments where she could serve him.

She was reborn about A.D. 900 into a poor family in Japan. She was forced to marry a man she did not love—the man she had killed in her previous life. He became a cripple and they lived in abject poverty, eating next to nothing. She pursued the only trade that she knew how to pursue. She became a prostitute, having to voluntarily give her body to many in order to serve the soul she had killed when he violated her body. Her service to him helped to expiate the karma of murdering him but didn't totally clear it.

She was reborn in Japan again at the end of that century and the man she married was the same soul as before. He was a taxidermist and supported the family while she served him as his wife. Even at the end of that lifetime, the karma of the murder was still not paid off.

Many incarnations later she was reborn in America in the twentieth century. She met this man again. He was the leader of a group in her church. They recognized each other's souls and her inner voice told her she needed to serve him. When she asked how, she was told to help with the church group. So she followed her inner voice in this and other instances and before too long they were married. She dropped out of college to support and serve him while he completed law school. A short ten months later, she was directed by this same inner voice to move on with her spiritual path. Her husband said it was a choice between him and the path. She replied that the choice was clear—her spiritual path.

Many days later she was cooking dinner in their small apartment and was cutting vegetables with a large knife. He was in the hallway and started an argument with her. Knife in hand, she walked out into the hallway, engaging in the argument. Then she looked at the knife and she looked at him. She dropped the knife, walked back into the kitchen and finished preparing the meal. She had come full circle to the original event. When she let go of the knife, she passed the test, fully balanced the karma and the relationship ended.

This is the true story of an extremely devoted student of the ascended masters. The murder was an isolated incident of darkness in the history of a very loving soul. But the story is a good example of how karma and reincarnation are inexorably linked.

Everyone has made both good and bad karma, and we have all had incarnations that set us back spiritually. By accepting this and taking responsibility for who we are and how we act, we will become much more loving and compassionate and less critical of ourselves and others—a great step forward in the soul's journey toward wholeness.

Desire—a Reincarnation Trap

Who is not familiar with the power of desire? Chapter 3 explored how difficult it is to gain mastery over the emotional, or desire, body. Desire is directly related to karma and reincarnation, which explains why souls reembody again and again. One of the clearest explanations of this issue can be found in the teachings of Buddhism.

Buddhist Teachings on Desire

After Gautama Buddha achieved enlightenment, he taught what is known as the First Noble Truth—that life is suffering. He was referring to suffering in the sense of being in an out-of-alignment state, out of line with universal law. He further said that the cause of suffering is desire—the Second Noble Truth. The two truths are intertwined.

Gautama Buddha

Gautama did not denounce all forms of desire but rather inordinate or wrong desire, a self-centered or selfish desire. The soul's main desire is to reunite with the Higher Self. When one identifies with the human self, he will suffer because he is out of alignment with the goal of ultimate reunion. Examples of inordinate or selfish desire might be the drive for personal aggrandizement, the greedy pursuit of pleasure or success, or addiction to a detrimental habit or substance. Such desires generate suffering because they build up the human self and take the soul away from its path.

Buddhism teaches that excessive and inordinate desires and passions are what cause people to reincarnate again and again. Until a person is free from desire, he cannot be free from the wheel of rebirth. Buddhist texts record the following quotes of Gautama on this subject:

> When he [anyone] fails to perceive the calamities due to sensual gratification and its fruition, and, being under the impression that sensuality is happiness, lives enthralled by his passions, he then begins to perform demeritorious karma.[16]

> When a man walks hand in hand with the thirst of craving, he will wander from birth to birth, now here, now there, and with never an end in sight.... The impulse "I want" and the impulse "I'll have"—lose them! That is where most people get stuck.[17]

> There is, in taking things, a thirst, a clinging, a grasping. You must lose it. You must lose it altogether, above, below, around and within. It makes no difference what it is you are grasping at: when a man grasps, Mara [the manifestation of illusion and evil] stands beside him. Therefore, the monks, realizing this, should not grasp at anything.[18]

16. Henry Clarke Warren, trans., *Buddhism in Translations* (1896; reprint, New York: Atheneum, 1969), p. 181.
17. H. Saddhatissa, trans., *The Sutta-Nipata* (1985; reprint, London: Curzon Press, 1987), p. 87.
18. Ibid., p. 127.

> When a person has assessed the world from top to bottom,... when there is nothing in the world that raises a flicker of agitation, then he has become a person free from the smoke-fumes, the tremblings and the hunger of desire. He has become calm. He has gone beyond getting old; he has gone beyond being born.[19]

Simply put, a soul is earthbound as long as she has inordinate desires and a longing to fulfill them. And fulfilling inordinate desires precipitates negative karma. So desire's connection to reincarnation is twofold. A soul reincarnates (1) to quench her desires and (2) to balance the negative karma she has made in acting out past desires. To help the soul break this wheel of rebirth and achieve her liberation, Gautama gives practical advice: free oneself from inordinate or wrong desire.

Excessive or Obsessive Desires

Not all desires are inordinate. Some types of desire move the soul in the direction of divine wholeness. For example, being passionate about fulfilling one's mission is a good thing. On the other hand, it is important to notice when a desire becomes excessive, because it may bring trouble. Some people do not recognize that they have an obsessive longing for something. Distinguishing between the types of motivation can be tricky, because desiring is a gray area compared to simply recognizing good or bad actions. A person can say to himself: "I should be able to have this. I should be able to have that. It's normal. It's the standard of living. If I want to do this, I should be able to do it."

One test to indicate if we are obsessive about a given desire is to note how attached we are to fulfilling it. Not being able to let go of a desire means that it's more than a passing thing; it's an attachment. The word *attachment* is key here, because through attachments to people, places, conditions and things, the seeker becomes fastened to this plane of existence. And therefore souls reincarnate again and again, pulled to the scenes of their unfulfilled desires.

In truth, some desires can literally lead us around by the nose. A common example would be an addiction to alcohol, drugs, tobacco, food or anything where a particular craving rules one's life. Other examples could be subtler but no less common, such as an overriding desire to look good, have powerful influence, or be greatly appreciated. When one notices such desires it is good to take action to begin clearing them away. The existence of organizations like Alcoholics Anonymous shows that society also recognizes and supports the positive action of freeing ourselves from such immoderate desires.

Keys for Overcoming Inordinate Desires

Here are two suggestions for recognizing and clearing away inordinate desires and attachments.

---

19. Ibid., p. 120.

> *You see, beloved ones, all desires of the human that you may have in this world can be surrendered. And when they are surrendered, the divine desiring of God comes into your life. For every human desire there is a divine desire that is legitimate, that is fulfilling, that will give to you whatever you thought you might get through human desiring but truly could never have or keep and much, much more. But it takes courage.*[20]
>
> —THE ASCENDED MASTER SAINT GERMAIN

1. **Make God-consciousness your first priority.**

    - Consider your desires in light of the first commandment that God gave to Moses: "I am the LORD thy God. . . . Thou shalt have no other gods before me."[21] Ask yourself the question, "What do I make my 'gods'?" Money? My job? My spouse? Success? Power? Good looks? Movies? The list could go on. This commandment serves to remind you of your innate divinity. Desires that help you to be the hands and feet of your Higher Self are fitting desires.

    - Similarly, it is good to ponder these words of Jesus: "Seek ye first the kingdom of God and his righteousness, and all these things shall be added unto you."[22] The ascended masters have taught that the true meaning of the word *king* is "***k***ey to the ***in***carnation of ***G***od" and that the Holy Christ Self is the king of our being, the one we want to be the ruler of our life. So you can consider whether or not your desires are in tune with the righteousness of your Christ Self and are ultimately leading you to the kingdom of higher consciousness. Desires are lawful if they do not pull you away from your soul's journey but take you toward the destination. If your first desire is to have the fullness of your Christ consciousness, then all your other needs will automatically be fulfilled.

2. **Give violet-flame decrees and affirmations.** The violet flame not only helps to clear away negative karma but also helps to transmute inordinate desire. Both are fundamental to the soul attaining union with the Divine and being liberated from the rounds of rebirth.

---

20. *Pearls of Wisdom,* vol. 27, no. 49, p. 422.
21. Exodus 20:2, 3.
22. Matthew 6:33.

EXERCISE: FREEING YOURSELF FROM INORDINATE DESIRES

Taking note of your desires can be practical and helpful. Decide if a given desire is propelling you higher or keeping you identified with the human consciousness. Every time you free yourself from an inordinate desire, you move one step closer towards soul liberation. Repeating this exercise periodically will help keep your desires in proper perspective.

Part 1: Taking a Look at Your Desires

1. Take some time to reflect on your various desires in life, recording these thoughts in your journal. To help with this process, write or mentally fill in the blanks in the following sentence.

   "I desire ____________________ so that ____________________."

   For example, you might say:

   I desire to eat so that I can keep my body healthy, or
   I desire to eat so that I can relish the taste of food.

   Another example might be:

   I desire money so that I can meet the needs of my family, or
   I desire money so that I can live a lavish lifestyle.

   Sentences like these can help point out if certain desires are assisting your soul to fulfill her path or if they are inordinate and based on attachment or selfishness. To get started, think about money, food, sex, power, fame and good looks. Also consider your desire for intangibles such as harmony, peace, love, and serving others. As you compile your list, let your thoughts come freely and do not make judgments about what you are writing down.

2. Continue until you have exhausted the list of your desires. Then look back over the list and decide which, if any, of these desires are inordinate or arouse a feeling of grasping or attachment within you. Referring to the previous section, "Keys for Overcoming Inordinate Desires," may help with this decision-making process.

Part 2: Meditation on the Violet Flame

1. Open your meditation with the following prayer:

   Beloved I AM Presence and Holy Christ Self, please free me from attachment to those desires that separate me from you, especially ____________________.

   (In the blank, name any inordinate desires that surfaced in Part 1.)

2. Now visualize yourself as the lower figure in the Chart of Your Divine Self surrounded by the violet flame. The violet flame can help clear away all attachment to those desires. As you give the following decree, imagine the violet flame purifying your consciousness and gradually dissolving those desires. Joyously invoke the action of the violet flame as you give the following decree three times. Since this decree also puts on your tube of light, please stand.

Soul in Physical Form

Beloved I AM Presence bright,
Round me seal your tube of light
From ascended master flame
Called forth now in God's own name.
Let it keep my temple free
From all discord sent to me.

I AM calling forth violet fire
To blaze and transmute all desire,
Keeping on in freedom's name
Till I AM one with the violet flame.

3. Close your meditation with the following prayer:

Beloved I AM Presence and Holy Christ Self, help me to always be in tune with your consciousness and to constantly move toward union with you. Free me from all wrong desires and replace them with desire for the Divine. According to God's will let it be done. Amen.

The Moral of the Story

We may or may not remember any of our past lives. We may or may not believe in reincarnation. None of that alters its validity. The ascended masters consider belief in reincarnation so important as to be the "keystone in the arch of being." What they mean is that without the understanding and acceptance of the truth of reincarnation, we cannot really understand our soul's path of evolution toward union with the I AM Presence—our very reason for being.

Reincarnation is the gateway to individual self-actualization in the highest sense of the word. When we correctly understand and accept the reality of the process of reembodiment we can develop a sense of the continuity of life—past, present and future. We are better equipped to see behind the surface of today's circumstances to the underlying karmic causes in our personal story that stretches back across the centuries. We begin to understand that the stories of our lives tie together and that they have a moral.

The moral of the story is that we can become one with our Higher Self. We can realize the fullness of divine consciousness where we are. But we have to strive to do our best. And in our striving, we can almost hear the hosts of heaven cheering for each one of us: Keep on keeping on until you make it! You *will* graduate from earth's schoolroom! You *will* fulfill your soul's reason for being! You *will* make your ascension!

> *"Don't worry if you don't believe in reincarnation. You'll get a second chance."*
>
> —ANONYMOUS

Meet Archangel Michael

Heaven's response to our heartfelt entreaties often comes borne on the wings of angels. Archangel Michael is one such marvelous being of light. We can quickly call to him for assistance in times of need and he will protect us as we carry out our spiritual and physical work. Archangel Michael's help is just a call away—why not simply ask for it?

Call to Archangel Michael for Help

Almost everyone has heard angel stories. Angels pull people back from the edges of cliffs and out of the paths of oncoming trains. They warn people in dangerous situations. They even protect those in tough neighborhoods.

Archangel Michael

God created the angels to serve and minister to us. Answering our prayers is their reason for being. Although we live in the material world, we have a special link to God through his angels. And we each have a divine spark within that allows us to ask the angels for help—and to expect results! The angels are literally waiting for us to give them assignments, for there is one rule they seldom break. Because we have free will, they don't intervene in our world unless we ask them to.

One of these servants of light is Archangel Michael, whose name means "who is like God." Archangel Michael is the greatest and most revered angel in Jewish, Christian and Islamic tradition. He serves on the first ray of the spiritual spectrum and we call to him especially for protection. The color we think of when we call to him is the color of the first ray, a vibrant blue.

We can ask Archangel Michael for practical assistance of all kinds. He can keep us from encountering physical and spiritual dangers, including everything from traffic accidents to falling into harmful habits. Archangel Michael can also help us gain freedom from fear and self-doubt. And he can help us to strengthen our faith, perfect our souls and fulfill our mission.

Anyone can benefit from calling to Archangel Michael. The call can be as simple as "Archangel Michael, help me, help me, help me!" This type of quick plea is especially good in car mishaps. When we use it, Archangel Michael can quickly summon help from a passerby in the event of car trouble, and he has helped save many lives in car wrecks.

Stories abound of intercessory action by Archangel Michael. Take Alex, who lost control of his car on an icy road. As he slid toward a precipice, he called to Archangel Michael. His car immediately moved back into the middle of the road. He said it was "almost as if it had been pushed by hand."

There is a potent decree to Archangel Michael called "Traveling Protection" which is designed specifically to help while we are traveling. It can be given whenever we get into our car to protect us as we drive from place to place or while walking, riding a bicycle or taking a plane. It is also a good decree to give in the morning after putting on our tube of light as added protection against accidents or negative incidents of any kind.

In "Traveling Protection," Archangel Michael is addressed as "Lord Michael." The masters sometimes refer to him and other heavenly beings as "Lord" out of respect for the high degree of divine consciousness that they have attained.

SPOKEN WORD PRACTICE: PROTECT YOURSELF WHILE TRAVELING

The "Traveling Protection" decree can make full use of your visualization skills. It works most effectively when you visualize Archangel Michael in the physical locations mentioned: before you, behind you, to your right, to your left, above you, beneath your feet and wherever you go.

www.SummitLighthouse.org/SA1-12

If visualization is a new practice for you or if it does not come easily, visualizing the directions could be a challenge. One technique that may be helpful is to extend your arm in the various directions indicated. So when you say, "Lord Michael before," extend your right arm out in front of you. Then with the words "Lord Michael behind," you turn so that your arm stretches out behind you, and so forth for the other directions. This technique is also very effective when instructing children to give this decree. They can benefit greatly from asking for Archangel Michael's protection before they go out to play or go to school, and they really enjoy the physical movements.

1. Find a quiet place and stand or sit comfortably.
2. Center your attention in your heart. Experience a deep sense of love for someone close to you by recalling a favorite event or scene. Stay with that feeling for a few moments.
3. Look at the picture of Archangel Michael. Then close your eyes and see this picture in your mind. Visualize Archangel Michael in the directions indicated by the decree as you say the words, using arm movements if you desire.
4. Give the body of the decree three times.

TRAVELING PROTECTION

www.SummitLighthouse.org/SA1-12

(Preamble)

In the name of the beloved mighty victorious Presence of God, I AM in me, my very own beloved Holy Christ Self, Holy Christ Selves of all mankind and beloved Archangel Michael, I decree:

(Decree Body)

Lord Michael before,
Lord Michael behind,
Lord Michael to the right,
Lord Michael to the left,
Lord Michael above,
Lord Michael below,
Lord Michael, Lord Michael wherever I go!

I AM his love protecting here!
I AM his love protecting here!
I AM his love protecting here!

(Closing)

And in full faith I consciously accept this manifest, manifest, manifest! (3x) right here and now with full power, eternally sustained, all-powerfully active, ever expanding and world enfolding until all are wholly ascended in the light and free!

Beloved I AM! Beloved I AM! Beloved I AM!

Archangel Michael

CHAPTER 7

Your Ultimate Destiny

Ascending Back to Spirit

The ascension is literally the final stage in the process of becoming an ascended being. The ascended masters have not only outlined the requirements for the supreme union with the divine, but have also left the victorious footprints of their lives for us to follow. To help us better identify with how the ascension relates to our personal spiritual path, it is helpful to understand the steps on the path to this glorious goal: how the soul becomes bonded to her Holy Christ Self, the major requirements for making one's ascension, and the hallmarks of the culminating ritual.

> *The entire effort of our Soul is to become God. This effort is as natural to man as that of flying is to birds.*[1]
>
> —MARSILIO FICINO (fourteenth-century philosopher and theologian)

The Goal of Life: The Ascension

Imagine yourself with the appearance of eternal youth, no longer concerned with age, disease or ill health. You look like a joyous young adult. You can bring physical objects into manifestation by the power of your will. You can travel from one place to another by just thinking about it. You can appear in several locations at once. You are united in brotherhood with all beings in the universe. You are an ascended master or lady master, an individual who has successfully pursued a path of spiritual evolution, achieved mastery over time and space, and united with your I AM Presence.

> *Lo, I AM everywhere in the consciousness of God!*[2]
>
> —THE ASCENDED MASTER LANELLO

The spiritual path here on earth leads to the ultimate goal of the ascension. In the beginning, we were one with our I AM Presence in higher realms of the heaven-world. We descended for a purpose and a mission and were given free will. In the process of the journey, we made mistakes, forgetting who we were and where we came from. We are slowly working our way back to our reunion with God. The ascension is our ticket home—our entrée into heaven forever.

The ascension is a spiritual acceleration of consciousness that occurs after the natural conclusion of one's final lifetime on earth. It represents the point in the soul's evolution when she attains immortality. Through the ascension, the soul merges with the I AM Presence and returns to the Father-Mother God, free from the rounds of karma and reincarnation. This process of returning to the source is recognized throughout the world's major religions, although the terminology used to describe it may differ.

1. Marsilio Ficino, quoted in Paul Oskar Kristeller, *The Philosophy of Marsilio Ficino*, trans. Virginia Conant (New York: Columbia University Press, 1943).
2. *Pearls of Wisdom*, vol. 16, no. 31, p. 131.

For example, a Hindu text speaks of the soul's return using the metaphor of fire. The Mundaka Upanishad teaches: "This is the truth: As from a fire aflame thousands of sparks come forth, even so from the Creator an infinity of beings have life and to him return again."[3] Taoism refers to the eternal Tao as being the mother of the world. Lao Tzu said we return to her at the conclusion of our earthly existence:

> The world has a beginning
> that is the mother of the world.
> Once you've found the mother,
> thereby you know the child.
> Once you know the child,
> you return to keep the mother,
> not perishing though the body die....
> Using the shining radiance,
> you return again to the light,
> not leaving anything to harm yourself.
> This is called entering the eternal.[4]

Bonding with the Holy Christ Self and I AM Presence

As one makes progress on the spiritual path, he comes closer and closer to his Holy Christ Self. Through a gradual increase in higher consciousness and self-transcendence, he can eventually achieve what is known as the bonding to the Christ Self. This bonding is a precursor to the ascension, when the soul is united with the I AM Presence. The bonding process is called the "alchemical marriage," because through it the seeker becomes one with the Christ. This marriage means there is no separation between the soul and the Holy Christ Self—the two have become joined. When this occurs, the student walks the earth as a Christed, or anointed, one.

Chart of Your Divine Self

In the Chart of Your Divine Self just above the head of the Christ, a dove is pictured descending from the I AM Presence. This dove represents the essence of love, the Holy Spirit, bestowing the graces of the Father-Mother God upon the Christ Self and on the soul as she increasingly bonds with the Holy Christ Self. As the soul's consciousness merges with that of her Christ Self, she also becomes one with the universal Christ consciousness.

Bonding with our Holy Christ Self means that our soul has raised the vibration of her consciousness to the level of the Christ consciousness. Because of this new congruency, our Christ consciousness is no longer above us—in vibration—as it appears in the chart. It has descended to occupy our form in matter. The chart can be seen as a chronological diagram of ourselves—past, present and future. One day we are the lower self. At a future point in time, we become one with our

3. Juan Mascaro, trans., *The Upanishads* (London: Penguin Books, 1965), p. 77.
4. Thomas Cleary, trans. and ed., *Vitality, Energy, Spirit: A Taoist Sourcebook* (Boston: Shambhala Publications, 1991), p. 15.

Christ Self. And sometime later, we are embraced by the arms of our I AM Presence through the ritual of the ascension.

Becoming fused to the Holy Christ Self frees one to think, act and deal with daily challenges from the perspective of that divine mediator. He becomes empowered through the Christ Self to love others in a more pure and complete way. Life here on earth becomes a much closer approximation of divine reality. It is "as Above, so below." The ascended masters teach that the closer the individual comes to God, the more sharply defined is his individuality. The very specific qualities and skills that make a person unique have been developed over many lifetimes. Bonding to the Holy Christ Self allows for a fuller manifestation of the godlike personality that the soul created through freewill choices.

We Ascend Daily

The ascension process follows the natural course of spiritual evolution. The Ascended Master Lanello tells us, "You ascend daily!"[5] Each day life tests the seeker. All of the thoughts, feelings and deeds from the present and past lives count toward or against the ascension. In taking progressive steps on the spiritual path, one ultimately finds his way back to the heart of God and enters the eternal life. In the end, success depends on the individual. The Ascended Master Serapis Bey expresses this idea well: "You need not expect, precious ones, that as the swoop of a great bird of paradise, heaven will come down to you and raise you instantly up into the light. Each day you weave a strand of light substance back to the heart of your Presence by the shuttle of your attention; each strand strengthens the anchor beyond the veil and thus draws you into a state of consciousness wherein God can use you more as an effective instrument for good."[6]

The ascension process is like the ascent up a pyramid. In Egypt and parts of Mexico, including the Yucatan peninsula, a person can spend days climbing the ruins of the pyramids, with each step taking him closer to the top. The pyramid the aspirant climbs daily is not made of stone but of light, the pure essence of divinity. It is the pyramid of the ascension. Thoughts, feelings and actions are all steps by which he climbs toward the apex of this pyramid. Approaching the top, the pyramid's steps grow narrower and the climber must be more and more careful as he approaches the goal.

Ascending the steps does not happen all at once but rather on an incremental basis. Life is not always a constantly ascending process. In other words, the seeker may not climb steadily up the pyramid each and every day. Perhaps there is a pause to catch his breath. Or the climber may actually

5. *Pearls of Wisdom,* vol. 35, no. 10, p. 120.
6. Serapis Bey, *Dossier on the Ascension: The Story of the Soul's Acceleration into Higher Consciousness on the Path of Initiation* (Gardiner, Mont.: Summit University Press, 1978), pp. 166–67.

stumble and slide down a step or two. There may even be times when he feels he is not moving upward at all. But progress eventually resumes and he is on his way again. In the same way, steady upward movement will eventually lead the aspirant toward the wonderful divine union with Spirit.

Although progress may sometimes seem intangible, it is helpful to remember that we are on earth because our karma dictates that this is the best place to be. It is appropriate to consider ourselves as unascended beings striving to make our ascension. The messenger Mark Prophet said that we have to recognize that if God wanted us up in heaven right this minute, we would be there and not here. We are on earth because the most practical place for us to be in our present state of evolution is in physical embodiment. We have lessons to learn. We have spiritual responsibilities and material challenges to master. And we must fulfill our mission as Christ fulfilled his.

> *The ascension is the fulfillment of the will of God for every man.*[7]
> —THE ASCENDED MASTER SERAPIS BEY

Ascended Masters

When you become an ascended master, you pass from time and space into infinity. After the ascension, you have the freedom to move through higher dimensions and to create, learn and love as never before. The ascension also signals the end of the need to reincarnate. With the ascension, a whole new world of spiritual existence opens up. You can perform cosmic service in ascended-master octaves, or teach and assist the people of earth.

Many historical figures have passed through the ascension. Great avatars as well as ordinary people have achieved this magnificent goal of life. Jesus Christ demonstrated the process of the ascension so that all could follow his example. His ascension is recorded in the Gospel of Luke: "And he led them out as far as to Bethany, and he lifted up his hands and blessed them. And it came to pass, while he blessed them, he was parted from them and carried up into heaven."[8]

The Bible mentions several other people who have ascended into the light. Among these is Enoch, who "walked with God and he was not, for God took him."[9] Elijah the prophet "went up by a whirlwind into heaven," having been parted from Elisha by a chariot and horses of fire.[10] Among the many ascended masters from Judeo-Christian tradition whose ascensions are not noted historically are Melchizedek, Mary the Mother of Jesus, Jesus' disciple John, St. Thérèse of Lisieux and Padre Pio.

Many great souls from the East have also ascended, such as Krishna, Zarathustra and Gautama Buddha. While they were in embodiment, these remarkable teachers founded major religions based on eternal truths. Millions and millions

7. Mark L. Prophet and Elizabeth Clare Prophet, *Lords of the Seven Rays: Mirror of Consciousness*, Book One (Gardiner, Mont.: Summit University Press, 1986), p. 175 (2011 reprint, p. 162).
8. Luke 24:50, 51.
9. Genesis 5:24.
10. II Kings 2:11.

of people follow these ascended masters as celebrated spiritual leaders, but few people, East or West, actually recognize the ascension as a daily process and an immediate goal of life on earth.

Most people who have ascended have had many incarnations. They spent many lifetimes in service to God and man. By studying their lives and their teachings, we can follow their example and return to our origin, too.

Zarathustra

Unascended Masters

When the opportunity for the ascension comes, you can choose to take your ascension or to enter into another round of service on the physical plane. The messenger Mark L. Prophet faced this choice at the conclusion of his life in 1973. After his death, he consulted with several ascended masters on the etheric plane as to whether or not he should ascend. He made the decision to take his ascension because it would provide him with a greater opportunity to serve his loved ones and souls of light throughout the world.

There are some advanced souls in embodiment today who at some point in the past were ready to make their ascension but chose to reembody on earth because of their dedication to those who still needed assistance. Some of these unascended masters have taken a vow and said: "I will not take my ascension, I will not take my leave of the planet, until every last man, woman and child is free."

Some unascended masters living in the mountains and caves of the Himalayas have made this commitment. They are present to hold a spiritual focus of light for the earth. Other unascended masters minister to life in other ways. So when it is time for you to take your ascension, you may choose either to ascend or to remain in embodiment to continue serving humanity.

Himalayas

The Ritual of the Ascension

The ascension is truly a marvelous event because it elevates the consciousness of the entire planet when it occurs. When one soul achieves her victory, other souls are magnetized to accelerate on their path to the ascension. When many ascensions take place in any given year, all of humanity becomes more receptive to divine inspiration. At that time, developments in all fields, such as science, education and healing, are quickened.

We are presently living in a special time period where the ascended masters can actively teach those who are spiritually receptive to prepare them for this great goal. The masters have told us that there will be mass ascensions from the hillsides in this age. Those who catch this wave of spiritual acceleration will find that getting to the shore of the ascension is a real possibility.

When someone earns the right to make his ascension, all of the light he has accumulated is accelerated in a process of spiritual transformation. His atoms, cells and chakras quicken, and he returns in dramatic splendor to the sun of the

I AM Presence. Individuals can ascend in one of two ways. They can ascend physically or they can ascend at inner spiritual levels, using their etheric bodies.

The Physical Ascension

In the physical ascension, the atoms of the body are accelerated until the physical form becomes a glorified spiritual body. The physical ascension requires balancing 95 to 100 percent of one's karma while still in embodiment. Therefore, it is the exception to the rule. Those who are intended to ascend physically must have had many thousands of years of preparation. Most souls pass on through the natural death of the physical body and make their ascension at spiritual levels from an etheric temple of the ascended masters.

The physical ascension of David Lloyd, the son of a British officer stationed in India, has been described by Godfré Ray King, pen name for Guy Ballard. Ballard served as a messenger for the ascended masters in the 1930s. In his book *Unveiled Mysteries*[11] he records the following story.

At the age of twenty, David Lloyd received an intriguing communication from an unascended master. He was told that when he found a man on a great mountain in North America who would offer him a crystal cup of sparkling liquid, that person would assist him in making his ascension.

Despite extremely difficult trials, disappointments and sorrows, David Lloyd continued his search for fifty years until he happened upon Godfré Ray King on Mount Shasta in California. Lloyd told Godfré the remarkable story of his life. At some point, Godfré felt the power of his I AM Presence come over him and in his hand materialized a crystal cup filled with living, liquid light. David Lloyd drank its contents and Godfré grasped both of David's hands in his own. At that moment all traces of age disappeared from David and he began to rise from the earth. His clothes vanished and he was clad in glistening white garments. He then disappeared in a stream of radiant light.

Later in a dictation, this newly ascended master described his inner experience of what had taken place physically:

> So wondrous was...that caress of the infinite upon my finite being.... The perfect body appeared. The perfect mind appeared. The perfect soul ruled the world of my being. A surge of infinite strength came forth and I rose into the air....
>
> For a cloud... of infinite, cosmic love received me out of the sight of men. And in the bond of cosmic compassion, I expanded my knowledge into the infinite as cadences of loveliness, receding into a far and distant future, which appeared before me then as a mountain of hope. And I entered in to the joy of God. And the joy of God filled my soul, and darkness vanished altogether.

11. Godfré Ray King, *Unveiled Mysteries* (Chicago: Saint Germain Press, 1982).

> And in the mystery of being, I understood that others like me would follow also in the wake of my experience and would come to realize at last that the infinite lamp of God was always lit, awaiting the return home of the prodigal child and the lifting up of each individual who passed through this magnificent gift of attainment with the vestments of immortality.
>
> Oh, what joy filled my being! After all these years, home at last.... Praise unto God swelled up within me, and the passions of holy prayer, even from this higher state [began] to peal, first like distant thunder and then with increasing cadences and power until my soul could scarcely stand the completeness of this joy as it cascaded within me....
>
> One day that of which you have scarcely dreamed will become for you, as for me, a tender reality, an infinite gift—the gift of infinity.... Understand that it is the loving plan of God for each of you to be raised into the ritual of your ascension in due process of time, when the fullness of the time has come.[12]

The physical ascension produces great changes in the body of the ascending person. A graphic description of this outer transformation is given by the Ascended Master Serapis Bey in the book *Dossier on the Ascension*:

> It is true, although the form of an individual may show signs of age prior to his ascension, that all of these signs will change and that the physical appearance of the individual will be transformed into the glorified body. The individual ascends, then, not in an earthly body but in a glorified spiritual body into which the physical form is changed on the instant by total immersion in the great God flame.
>
> Thus man's consciousness of the physical body ceases and he achieves a state of weightlessness. This resurrection takes place as the great God flame envelops the shell of human creation that remains and transmutes, in a pattern of cosmic grids, all of the cell patterns of the individual—the bony structure, the blood vessels, and all bodily processes which go through a great metamorphosis.
>
> The blood in the veins changes to liquid golden light; the throat chakra glows with an intense blue-white light; the spiritual eye in the center of the forehead becomes an elongated God flame rising upward; the garments of the individual are completely consumed, and he takes on the appearance of being clothed in a white robe—the seamless garment of the Christ. Sometimes the long hair of the Higher Mental Body appears as pure gold on the ascending one; then again, eyes of any color may become a beautiful electric blue or a pale violet....
>
> Whether it be Zarathustra, who ascended back to God in "the great flame," or Elijah who went into heaven in the "chariot of fire"—the

Holy Christ Self

12. Dictation by the Ascended Master David Lloyd, December 30, 1970.

> flame of the ascension is the key which unlocks the door to immortality for every man. The flame is the vehicle which conveys the ascended one back to the heart of his Divine Presence. He retains full consciousness of this entire ritual and, once ascended, he becomes on the instant an emissary of the Great White Brotherhood in carrying out its various aims which always come under the direction of the Fatherhood of God.[13]

Truly the physical ascension is an impressive phenomenon. However, a person who makes a nonphysical ascension ends up the same as the one who physically ascends—as an ascended master.

Ascending from Inner Levels

People who ascend at inner spiritual levels do so from a focus of the ascended masters on the etheric plane, or heaven-world, called a retreat. Etheric retreats have a physical coordinate on earth but cannot usually be seen because they exist in spiritual realms. Those who are prepared to make their ascension at the close of their final embodiment go to an etheric retreat to receive the initiation that will reunite them with their God Presence. Many people ascend from the etheric retreat of the Ascension Temple focused at Luxor, Egypt, and participate in the following ascension ritual.

Accompanied by ascended masters and highly evolved souls, the ascending soul enters a room called the "flame room" and stands on a dais in the center of a large circle with ascended masters and angelic hosts, with her brothers and sisters of light gathered on the outside of the circle. At a certain moment when all is in readiness, a cosmic tone that is uniquely hers is sounded and a current from above the candidate is released from a circle on the ceiling while a current from below rises from the base. The moment this tone is rung out, a flame formed by the caduceus action of both currents bursts forth, and the angelic hosts in the outer court trumpet the victory of the ascending soul with a magnificent rendition of the "Triumphal March" from the opera *Aïda*. The ascension currents then surround and transform the etheric body of the ascending one into the perfection required for union with the I AM Presence.

Ascension Temple at Luxor

The ascension is truly a grand and glorious event that signals the culmination of lifetimes of striving to manifest one's innate divinity. As one gradually garners light in his being through correct thoughts, words and deeds, he is brought successfully to this final point of victory. Making the ascension also entails that several key requirements are met.

13. Serapis Bey, *Dossier on the Ascension*, pp. 176–78.

> *The future is what you make it, even as the present is what you made it. If you do not like it, God has provided a way for you to change it; and the way is through the acceptance of the currents of the ascension flame.*[14]
>
> —THE ASCENDED MASTER SERAPIS BEY

Requirements for the Ascension

The requirements for the ascension are essential ingredients of the spiritual path. They are preparatory steps that help purify the soul and get her ready for this major transformation. The following is a brief overview of these steps.

The soul must meet several conditions in order to ascend. The three primary ones are (1) balancing her threefold flame, (2) fulfilling her mission on earth according to her divine plan and (3) balancing at least 51 percent of her karma. These requirements are covered in detail in this chapter.

The other prerequisites for the ascension include aligning the four lower bodies, achieving self-mastery on the seven spiritual rays and attaining mastery over sin, sickness and death. The karmic records and patterns that fill the electronic belt must be transmuted, as well. And the Mother energy of the kundalini, the white light focused in the base-of-the-spine chakra, must be raised.

All of these requirements are somewhat interdependent because progress in one of them contributes to fulfilling the others. For example, balancing the threefold flame and balancing karma play a significant role in being able to successfully fulfill one's mission in life.

Balance Your Threefold Flame

Because the threefold flame is the link to the heart of the I AM Presence, it is a major key to spiritual progress. Balancing the threefold flame means that all the plumes are equally developed in size and capacity. It indicates that the love of one's heart is equal to the wisdom of his mind, and that both of these are equal to the determination of the divine will within.

The threefold flame is like the soul's motor—through it comes the spiritual drive for the chakras and four lower bodies. A motor will not work if it's not in balance. The motor in the heart also needs balance in order to work correctly. If the threefold flame is not balanced, some innate qualities become stronger than others and the aspirant gets lopsided in his spiritual evolution. When the threefold flame is in a state of imbalance, a sort of giantism can occur where one or two of the plumes is out of proportion to the others. This state can hinder the quest for individual Christ-mastery. Balance is the key.

Take the hypothetical example of a professor who is very much into his books and theoretical knowledge. His yellow plume will be quite well developed

14. Ibid., p. 89.

because he is good at studying. But because he is so wrapped up in intellectual pursuits, he may become unconcerned with the practical world of people and their needs. It does not occur to him to ask how to help them. He just does his work and thinks: "Well, I'm excellent in my field. I don't have to do anything else. Things are fine for me right now, so why should I change?" The problem is that he is not actively discovering the balancing factors of love and power. Without these balanced elements in his life, he will not progress spiritually.

The Ascended Master Serapis Bey says: "When men fail to progress, it is always because there is imbalance in the threefold flame of life.... The will of God is a predominant third of the whole, but lacking the wisdom of God, the golden illumination of his supreme knowledge, even power is stifled of action. And without love, power and wisdom become but the brittleness of self-preservation. The balance of the threefold flame creates a pattern of the ascension for all."[15]

It is interesting to note that whatever plume of the threefold flame is the shortest represents the area in which there is the most karma. So, working toward developing that aspect also means balancing karma in that domain. Here are a few tips for balancing the threefold flame.

Tips for Balancing Your Threefold Flame

1. **Expand the shortest plume through right actions.** The Ascended Master Saint Germain said: "As the Buddha taught, the key to self-mastery is self-observation. And so it is with balancing your threefold flame. Your sensitivity to its plumes will enable you to determine when any of the three is out of balance."[16] The following guidelines can help determine which of your plumes is least developed. You can then act to correct the imbalance.

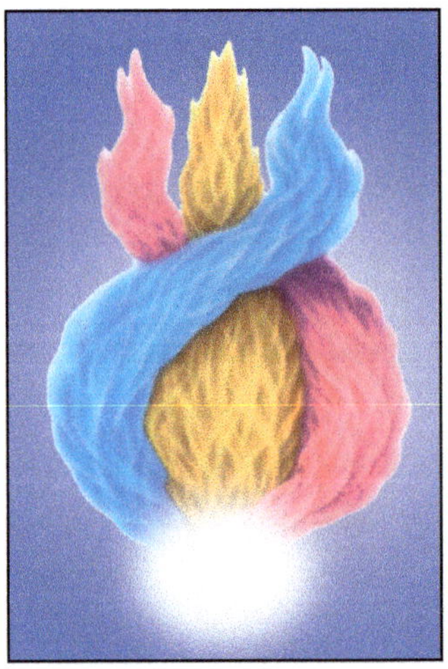

Threefold Flame

- The blue plume represents power, or dedication to the will of God. If you feel that you lack drive, desire or will, or if you don't seem to be able to get things done, you probably need to amplify the blue plume. One good way to do this is to take a leadership role you would not otherwise assume, since leadership offers the opportunity to correctly use power. Taking charge of a committee, leading a neighborhood drive for charity or organizing children's after-school activities can effectively increase the blue plume.

- The yellow plume represents wisdom and understanding. If you consistently avoid study or have difficulty understanding the ideas of other people, your yellow plume probably needs expanding. To strengthen this flame, you may wish to take up a course of study at night or teach the illiterate to read and write.

15. Serapis Bey, *Dossier on the Ascension,* p. 24.
16. *Pearls of Wisdom,* vol. 39, no. 30, p. 166.

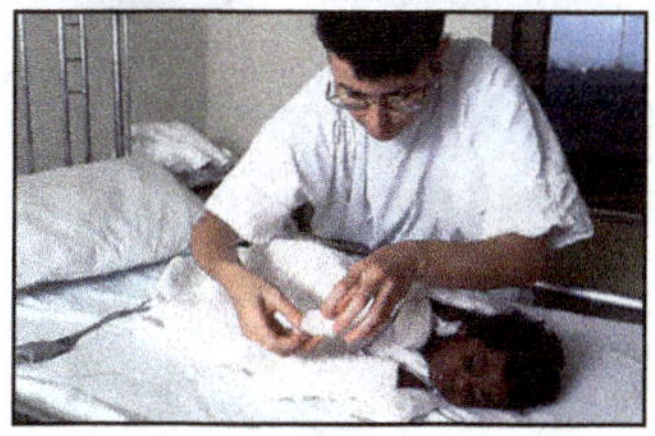

- The pink plume signifies love. If you have difficulty expressing love or feel that you don't love enough, then your pink flame could probably use a boost. One way to expand this plume is to actively do caring things for other people. You might look after neighborhood children, do odd jobs for those who are homebound, or do hospice work. Serving others always helps to amplify the flame of love.

2. **Give the decree "Balance the Threefold Flame in Me."** This decree can help to evenly balance all of the plumes of the threefold flame in your heart. Give it as frequently as you like to help achieve this goal. For a greater action, repeat the entire body of the decree three times.

BALANCE THE THREEFOLD FLAME IN ME

(Preamble)

In the name of the beloved mighty victorious Presence of God, I AM in me, my very own beloved Holy Christ Self and Holy Christ Selves of all mankind, I decree:

(Decree Body)

Balance the threefold flame in me! (3x)
Beloved I AM!
Balance the threefold flame in me! (3x)
Take thy command!
Balance the threefold flame in me! (3x)
Magnify it each hour!
Balance the threefold flame in me! (3x)
Love, wisdom and power!

(Closing)

And in full faith I consciously accept this manifest, manifest, manifest! (3x) right here and now with full power, eternally sustained, all-powerfully active, ever expanding and world enfolding until all are wholly ascended in the light and free!

Beloved I AM! Beloved I AM! Beloved I AM!

www.SummitLighthouse.org/
SA1-13

Fulfill Your Divine Plan

Another important requirement for the ascension is fulfilling the soul's divine plan, or inner blueprint. As stated in earlier chapters, everyone came forth from God with a special mission, a unique purpose to be accomplished on earth. That mission could be the calling to be a scientist, an artist, a minister or a saint. Whatever it is, the calling is a mandate to fulfill. Buddhists call this inner purpose the dharma.

One way to relate to your dharma, or mission, is to recognize where you have a passion in a certain area. This passion usually identifies itself as a burning desire within your being to do something that gives you special satisfaction. When you are living your passion, you are always thinking about it—from the time you wake up in the morning to the time you go to sleep at night. It is a passion that inspires you to do a job that you know is going to be for the betterment of your loved ones, the community or civilization—whether that means being a chef, coaching Little League, running for public office, or inventing something to help society.

Tips for Fulfilling Your Divine Plan

If you do not feel a sense of passion in anything that you are doing in life, you may find that one or more of the steps below can help you define that mission.

1. **Simplify and focus.** Streamline your life by setting spiritual and material priorities. To help you formulate this list of priorities, seriously ask yourself questions such as:

    - What is my greatest talent and how can I capitalize on it?
    - What is the greatest stumbling block to my spiritual progress and how can I get rid of it?
    - If money and time were no object, what would I do that would satisfy me the most?

    Write your priorities in your journal in descending order. Take steps to put your first priority into action by making a commitment. For example, if your first priority is to capitalize on your writing talent and you have never had training in that area, you might want to take some courses in writing. Revisit your list and action plans periodically as the priorities change.

2. **Examine yourself.** In your journal, make a list of inner desires, skills and talents. Also list your training and experience in areas that may help to fulfill your divine calling. Analyze this list to see if patterns emerge. Is the bulk of your talents, skills and experience in a single area? This may be the field in which you have a mission.

3. **Ask your Holy Christ Self to reveal your divine plan to you.** This can be in the form of a simple heartfelt call made in the quietude of each day, such as: "In the name I AM THAT I AM, beloved Holy Christ Self, reveal to me my divine plan, the mission that I am called to do in this life." Do this every day until you receive an answer.

4. **Take up the calling that you have discovered.** For instance, if you have determined that your mission is helping the homeless, then make it your priority to volunteer some time each week serving your local shelter. If fulfilling your mission requires a change in careers, get the training necessary to enable you to make the switch.

Balance 51 Percent of Your Karma

An essential requirement for the ascension is balancing 51 percent of one's karma by the conclusion of the final embodiment. Individuals used to be required to balance 100 percent of their karma, but this task was quite difficult. So the Lords of Karma determined that if one purifies 51 percent or more of all the energies that he has ever misqualified, he can ascend. Upon ascending, the remaining karma must be balanced from spiritual levels by giving the violet flame or by rendering service to earth and her evolutions.

Three important ways to balance karma in embodiment were covered in chapter 5. These are: (1) enduring it (2) serving life and (3) transmuting it with the violet flame. When you make it a priority to balance karma on a daily basis, you will find that you are able to fulfill this requirement much more easily.

MEDITATION ON YOUR ASCENSION

The following meditation is designed to help you tune into the vibration of the ascension flame. Doing it may cause you to experience a heightened desire for your own ascension. Feel free to repeat it as often as you like.

1. Find a quiet place where you will be undisturbed and sit in a comfortable position.
2. If possible, play some soft inspirational music.
3. Visualize yourself in the Ascension Temple at Luxor, Egypt.
4. See yourself as the candidate for the ascension, kneeling to receive the blessing of the Ascended Master Serapis Bey.
5. Visualize yourself being enfolded in the intense, fiery white flame of the ascension. Feel it envelop every aspect of your being in the purity of its dazzling light.
6. Give the following series of calls to anchor the flame of the ascension in your consciousness:

I claim the victory of my mission!
I claim the victory of my cosmic purpose and
my divine plan fulfilled!
I claim the victory in God's name!

www.SummitLighthouse.org/SA1-14

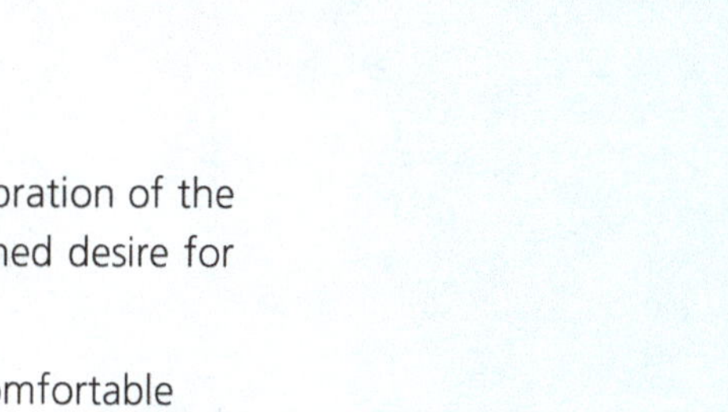

Ascension Temple at Luxor

I claim the victory of overcoming all within me
that is not the Christ consciousness!
I claim the victory of the light!
I claim the victory of the ascended masters' consciousness,
worlds without end!
I claim the victory of my ascension!

7. Now give the following decree three times:

I AM ascension light,
Victory flowing free,
All of good won at last
For all eternity.

I AM light, all weights are gone.
Into the air I raise;
To all I pour with full God power
My wondrous song of praise.

All hail! I AM the living Christ,
The ever-loving one.
Ascended now with full God power,
I AM a blazing sun!

8. Close your meditation with the following words:

Be sealed, my heart, in the heart of God!
Be sealed, my soul, in the heart of God!
Be sealed, my mind, in the heart of God!
Be sealed, my desire, in the heart of God!
Be sealed, my inner vision, in the heart of God!

You may also find it helpful to meditate on one or more of the following:

- The ascension flame, which has an intense, fiery white color with a crystal-like glow
- The Easter lily, the symbol of the ascension in the nature kingdom
- The diamond, the focus of the ascension in the mineral kingdom
- The "Triumphal March" by Verdi, the melody of the ascension flame

> *Immortality is of a high price, and it demands the allness of men from the smallness of men.*[17]
>
> —THE ASCENDED MASTER SERAPIS BEY

17. Prophet, *Lords of the Seven Rays,* Book One, p. 178 (2011 reprint, pp. 165–66).

Daily Decree to Archangel Michael

Creating a sacred space especially for your spiritual practices can enhance your experience. Giving your decrees and meditations in a location dedicated specifically to that purpose can build a powerful field of light-energy that makes your spiritual work easier and more enjoyable. Among the decrees you can give is a powerful new call to Archangel Michael, the great emissary of light discussed in the last chapter. This decree can establish a strong, blue-flame shield of protection around you as you go about your daily activities.

Creating a Sacred Space

It's a good idea to have a comfortable place where you can do your spiritual work without interruption. This place can be as simple as a chair in the corner of a room or it might be a whole room that is set aside for this purpose. It might even be a large closet where you can retreat and shut out distractions. Whatever area is available to you can become a hallowed space as you dedicate it to the pursuit of your sacred work. In fact, you may have already created such a place and are using it as your sanctuary from the hustle and bustle of daily life.

The purpose of the space is to assist you in communing with your divine nature, to raise your consciousness to a higher vibration, and to help the light to flow more freely through your chakras. You may choose to have a few simple things that help make it special for you:

- Objects from nature, like a special rock found on a nature walk, crystals or flowers (silk or live flowers are preferable)
- Books on topics relevant to your soul's journey
- Pictures or statues of angels or other objects that give you a sense of holiness
- A small altar with candles
- A fountain
- Photos of people or places that need your prayers, such as family members, whales, rain forests or the world
- Anything else that is meaningful to your individual path

The specific objects in your sacred space have an effect on the flow of energy in your surroundings. They can either help or hinder the descent of light invoked through your decrees. It is good to avoid any clutter that might hamper the free flow of energy. Ideally, all objects in this space should be relevant to your purpose of helping loved ones and the planet.

Studying spiritual teachings, practicing meditation and doing decrees are all activities that will infuse you and your surroundings with light. This divine energy will build over time and create what is called a "forcefield," or aura of energy, in your sacred space—just as your aura is the field of energy surrounding you. Similar forcefields of light can be experienced in great cathedrals, temples or mosques and in places like the Holy Land or the Great Pyramid in Egypt. They also occur in many beautiful areas of nature. In fact, the unimpeded flow of spiritual energy draws many people into nature as a place to nourish their souls.

You may also wish to enhance your space by using special lighting or burning incense. Or you may come up with other creative ideas of your own. Use your imagination. Just keep in mind that those things that are part of this space should be appropriate for the activity in which you are engaged. For example, background music might be counterproductive if you are giving decrees, but it might help you relax and absorb new material when you are reading. It may also be soothing for certain types of meditation.

If you already have a sacred space, you may wish to add to it or rearrange it. If you are just beginning to create such an atmosphere, have fun and attune to your soul's needs and how your surroundings can express your divine nature!

Using Support Materials

In addition to the resources listed under "Further Study" at the end of the book, information on valuable support materials can be obtained by ordering a free catalog from The Summit Lighthouse. Included in the catalog are books, booklets, DVDs, and CDs that can help you discover more about the science of the spoken Word and other relevant spiritual topics.

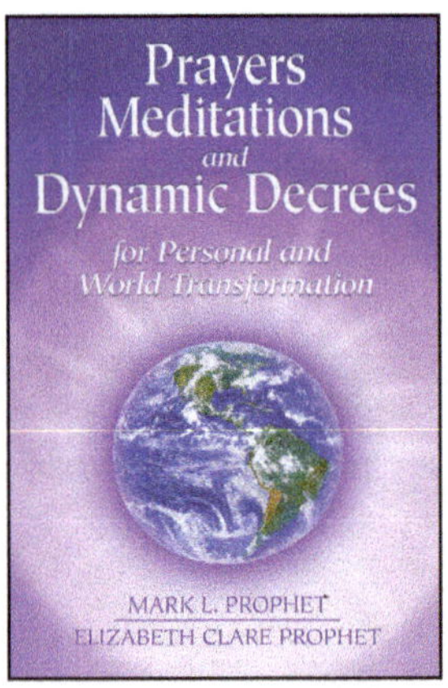

There is also a complete decree book—*Prayers, Meditations and Dynamic Decrees for Personal and World Transformation*—that contains all of the decrees currently available through The Summit Lighthouse. It has everything one needs to apply the science of the spoken Word to personal and world needs. Included are decrees for protection, wisdom, love, purity, abundance, healing, ministration, peace, forgiveness and transmutation. The decree book is color-coded in seven sections that correspond to the seven spiritual rays and chakras. Three-ring binders to hold these 7½" x 9" loose-leaf pages are also available.

A Decree to Protect You Each Day

The last chapter introduced you to Archangel Michael. When on a spiritual path it becomes important to call to Archangel Michael regularly because he can help you to stay focused on the goal of reunion with your Christ Self and I AM Presence. So, giving decrees to him for several minutes after invoking your tube of light is a wonderful practice to consider implementing. Archangel Michael even said that he would assign an angel to any person who decrees to him twenty minutes a day. This type of decree action can have remarkable benefits.

Take the case of Daniel, an airline pilot who decreed to Archangel Michael for about twenty minutes a day. One day he was taking his two young sons out for a tractor ride near their home outside Dallas, Texas, when a tree branch fell on his neck and back. With his back covered in blood, he was somehow able to drive the quarter mile back to his house. He didn't remember the drive, but four-year-old Christopher did. "Daddy drove the tractor home, but a big blue angel came down and sat on the front of the tractor," Christopher said. The angel told him that his daddy would be all right.

Daniel recovered quickly without surgery, although the hospital staff told him he was lucky not to be a quadriplegic. He believes his decrees enabled the angel to save him.

The following exercise uses heart centering and visualization as a preface to the decree to Archangel Michael. If you make this decree exercise a daily routine, you will find it to be an especially valuable habit!

SPOKEN WORD PRACTICE: SUGGESTED DAILY DECREE ROUTINE TO INVOKE ARCHANGEL MICHAEL'S PROTECTION

1. Go within and consciously draw all your attention to the point of your heart. It may help to close your eyes and place your hand over your heart.
2. Breathe deeply several times until you feel calm and centered.
3. Feel a deep sense of love for someone close to you by recalling a favorite event or scene.
4. Still focused in your heart, look at this picture of Archangel Michael.
5. Close your eyes and see his image in your mind. Visualize Archangel Michael standing over you as a tall, powerful being who completely envelops you in his presence.
6. Give the following decree to Archangel Michael to invoke his protection. After giving each verse followed by the refrain, give the coda three times. Then repeat the decree body in its entirety three times.

Archangel Michael over Devotee

www.SummitLighthouse.org/SA1-15

ARCHANGEL MICHAEL

In the name of the beloved mighty victorious Presence of God, I AM in me, my very own beloved Holy Christ Self, Holy Christ Selves of all mankind and beloved Archangel Michael, I decree:

1. Lord Michael, Lord Michael,
   I call unto thee—
   Wield thy sword of blue flame
   And now cut me free!

Refrain: Blaze God-power, protection
Now into my world,
Thy banner of faith
Above me unfurl!
Transcendent blue lightning
Now flash through my soul,
I AM by God's mercy
Made radiant and whole!

2. Lord Michael, Lord Michael,
   I love thee, I do—
   With all thy great faith
   My being imbue!

3. Lord Michael, Lord Michael
   And legions of blue—
   Come seal me, now keep me
   Faithful and true!

Coda: I AM with thy blue flame
Now full-charged and blest,
I AM now in Michael's
Blue-flame armor dressed! (3x)

And in full faith I consciously accept this manifest, manifest, manifest! (3x) right here and now with full power, eternally sustained, all-powerfully active, ever expanding and world enfolding until all are wholly ascended in the light and free!

Beloved I AM! Beloved I AM! Beloved I AM!

INVITATION

Thank you for sharing in the sacred adventure of *The Spiritual Quest.* Hopefully you've gleaned many keys to help you navigate life's ongoing spiritual journey. If this book has been helpful to you, book 2 in the series, *Meeting the Masters,* and book 3, *Working with the Masters,* offers exciting new frontiers for self-discovery and connecting with the heavenly hierarchy. To order these books or related products, see the "Further Study" section at the end of this book.

May your sacred adventure continue to be a joyous and insightful journey to the heights and depths of your soul and to the magnificent purpose that life has in store for you!

MY JOURNAL

Affirmation. A positive statement, usually beginning with the name of God, "I AM," that affirms and strengthens the qualities of God within oneself, helping to bring those qualities into physical manifestation.

Aquarian age. The 2,150-year cycle following the age of Pisces. The age of Pisces gave us the understanding of God as the Son, exemplified by the sponsor of that age, Jesus Christ. The age of Aquarius brings us the awareness of God as the Holy Spirit and as the Divine Mother. It is sponsored by the Ascended Master Saint Germain and his divine complement, the Ascended Lady Master Portia. During this cycle, the opportunity will be given to mankind to apply the laws of freedom and justice, the science of precipitation and transmutation, and rituals of invocation to God that can bring in an age of enlightenment and peace such as the world has never known.

Archangel Michael. The angel of the LORD who stands in defense of the Christ consciousness in all children of God; also known as the Prince of the Archangels and the Defender of the Faith. As the archangel of the first ray, Michael embodies the qualities of faith, protection, perfection and the will of God. He is the most revered angel in Jewish, Christian and Islamic scripture and tradition.

Archangel Raphael. Archangel of the fifth spiritual ray (green ray) of science, healing and vision. Archangel Raphael, together with Mother Mary, his divine complement, brings great healing energy to the evolutions of earth. In Hebrew, Raphael's name means "God has healed." The *Zohar* (a Jewish mystical text) says that "Raphael is charged by God to heal the earth, and through him the earth furnishes an abode for man, whom he also heals of his maladies."

Ascended masters. Enlightened spiritual beings who once lived on earth, fulfilled their reason for being and ascended, or reunited with God. The ascended masters are the true teachers of mankind, directing the spiritual evolution of all devotees of God.

Ascension. A spiritual acceleration of consciousness that takes place at the natural conclusion of one's final lifetime on earth whereby the soul reunites with God and is free from the rounds of karma and rebirth.

Astral body. One of the four lower bodies of man, also called the emotional, or desire, body. It records the emotions and contains the higher and lower desires.

Aum, Om. (Sanskrit) The sacred syllable of creation, the Word that went forth in the Beginning and from which all other sounds originated.

Aura. A luminous emanation or electromagnetic field that surrounds the physical body. The atmosphere surrounding and interpenetrating the four lower bodies of man and his chakras upon which the impressions, thoughts, feelings, words and actions of the individual are registered, including his karma and the records of past lives.

Base-of-the-spine chakra. Sanskrit name: *Muladhara,* meaning "root" and "base," or "foundation." A four-petaled white chakra located at the base of the spinal column. It is associated with the fourth ray and the expression of purity, hope, joy, self-discipline, integration, perfection, wholeness and nurturing.

Causal Body. Interpenetrating spheres of light surrounding each one's I AM Presence at spiritual levels. The spheres of the causal body contain the records of the virtuous acts we have performed to the glory of God and the blessing of man through our many incarnations on earth.

Chakra. (Sanskrit, meaning "wheel," "disc" or "circle") Term used to denote the centers of light anchored in the etheric body that govern the flow of energy to the four lower bodies of man.

Chohan. *Chohan* is a term that is used to mean "lord" or "master." A specific chohan presides over each of the seven rays. These seven chohans, or lords, of the rays have specialized in the application of their ray throughout their many incarnations on earth, and they can instruct us in self-mastery on that ray. The names of the chohans and their rays are as follows: El Morya, first ray; Lanto, second ray; Paul the Venetian, third ray; Serapis Bey, fourth ray; Hilarion, fifth ray; Nada, sixth ray; Saint Germain, seventh ray.

Christ consciousness. The consciousness or awareness of the self in and as the Christ; the attainment of a level of consciousness commensurate with that which was realized by Jesus, the Christ. The Christ consciousness is the realization within the soul of that mind which was in Christ Jesus.

Christhood. The individual expression of the universal Christ consciousness. On the spiritual path the individual Christ Self, the personal Christ, is the initiator of the soul. When the individual passes certain initiations on the path of Christhood, he or she earns the right to be called a Christed one and gains the title of Son or Daughter of God.

Cosmos. Known also as Mighty Cosmos, he is an ascended master and cosmic being who has attained cosmic consciousness and literally holds the entire cosmos in his aura. He ensouls the energies of many worlds and systems of worlds within this galaxy and beyond with the power of the five secret rays.

Crown chakra. Sanskrit name: *Sahasrara,* meaning "thousandfold." A golden-yellow chakra of 972 petals located at the crown of the head. It is associated with the second ray and the expression of illumination, wisdom, self-knowledge, understanding, humility, open-mindedness and cosmic consciousness.

Crystal cord. The stream of light, life and consciousness descending from the I AM Presence that nourishes and sustains the soul and her four lower bodies. Also called the silver cord.

Decree. A dynamic form of spoken prayer used by students of the ascended masters to direct God's spiritual energy into individual and world conditions to produce constructive change.

Dharma. (Sanskrit, literally "carrying," "holding," "that which holds one's true nature") An individual's dharma is his duty to fulfill his reason for being. It is his divine plan, which runs as a thread through all his lifetimes. When one's dharma is fulfilled and sufficient karma is balanced, the soul is eligible for the ascension.

Dictations. The messages of the ascended masters, archangels and other advanced spiritual beings delivered through the agency of the Holy Spirit by a messenger of the Great White Brotherhood.

Divine blueprint. The spiritual blueprint of life imprinted by God upon the fiery core of the I AM Presence. The divine blueprint contains one's divine plan and the keys to fulfilling his unique destiny.

Divine plan. The plan of God for the soul, ordained in the beginning when the blueprint of life was impressed upon the white-fire core of the individual I AM Presence. Each individual soul is destined to realize the fullness of her preordained (but not predestined) potential.

Divine Self. The Higher Self; the I AM Presence and Holy Christ Self; the exalted aspect of selfhood.

Djwal Kul. The ascended master known also as D.K. and "the Tibetan." He was the foremost disciple of Kuthumi and is said to have lived near his teacher in Tibet. Djwal Kul assisted Kuthumi and El Morya in their work with the Theosophical Society. He was also embodied as Caspar, one of the three wise men who honored Jesus at his birth.

Eighth ray. The ray of integration, whereby one integrates the mastery of the seven rays through the flame of the Christ, the threefold flame. The eighth ray corresponds to the secret chamber of the heart, an eight-petaled chakra behind and to the left of the heart chakra, where the threefold flame is sealed.

El Morya. Chohan of the First Ray, the blue ray, of divine power. He tutors souls in gaining self-mastery in the throat chakra and through developing faith, goodwill, leadership, protection, perfection and surrender to the divine will. El Morya counsels many types of people, including those who serve in the governments of the nations, teachers, scientists, economists, the avant-garde and servants of the will of God. He is the teacher and sponsor of Mark and Elizabeth Clare Prophet and founder of The Summit Lighthouse.

Electronic belt. The negative spiral or forcefield of density that a person creates through his misuses of energy in the present and in all past lives. Extending from the waist to beneath the feet, the electronic belt is similar in shape to a large kettledrum and contains the cumulative records of one's negative thoughts and feelings. It is the perversion of the causal body.

Elijah. The Israelite prophet who was taken up into heaven in a chariot of fire (II Kings 2:11). He later embodied as John the Baptist, who prepared the way for Jesus' mission (Matt. 17:10–13). Elijah was a rare exception of a man who ascended and then reembodied in physical form. After his lifetime as John the Baptist, he returned to the ascended state.

Elizabeth Clare Prophet. Mystic, writer, lecturer, spiritual teacher and messenger for the ascended masters—those who have walked a spiritual path and reunited with God. As messenger, she has produced a vast body of work in audio, video, book and lecture form. These works include more than 1,800 dictations from the ascended masters and more than 75 books on their teachings. She has been featured on such national TV shows as NBC's "In Search Of," and "Ancient Prophecies." She has also talked about her work on "Donahue" and "Larry King Live" and has lectured widely throughout the United States and in 28 countries, speaking on spiritual topics such as prophecy, the aura, reincarnation and the mystical paths of the world's religions.

Emotional body. One of the four lower bodies of man, also called the desire, or astral, body. It records the emotions and contains the higher and lower desires.

Enoch. According to the Bible, Enoch was a prophet who predicted the judgment of the ungodly (Jude 4–19). The Bible says that "Enoch walked with God and he was not, for God took him" (Gen. 5:24). This has been interpreted as the record of his ascension; he is now known as the Ascended Master Enoch.

Etheric body. Also called the memory body, it houses the blueprint of the soul's identity and contains the memory of all that has ever transpired in the soul and all impulses she has ever sent out.

Etheric plane. The highest plane or octave in the dimensions of matter; a plane that is as concrete and real as the physical plane, but that is experienced through the senses of the soul in a dimension and a consciousness beyond physical awareness.

Etheric retreat. A place of enormous spiritual light located in the etheric plane, or heaven-world, the highest vibrating plane in matter. Retreats consist of entire etheric cities, temples of light and structures with various rooms dedicated to specific purposes. Each retreat has unique characteristics and maintains a reserve of light-energy, which is used to help humanity on its evolutionary path. During sleep and between embodiments, the soul can travel to the retreats in her etheric body to receive in-depth instruction from members of the cosmic hierarchy.

Father-Mother God. The divine wholeness spoken of by the Lord Christ in Revelation as "the beginning and the ending," Alpha and Omega. Through the Universal Christ, the Word incarnate, the Father is the origin and the Mother is the fulfillment of the cycles of God's consciousness expressed throughout the Spirit-Matter creation.

Five secret rays. Light emanations of the Godhead that originate in the white-fire core of the causal body. They correspond to the five minor chakras, which are located in the hands, the feet and the left side of the chest.

Four lower bodies. The four sheaths surrounding the soul; the vehicles the soul uses in her journey on earth: the etheric, or memory, body; the mental body; the desire, or emotional body; the physical body.

Gautama Buddha. *Buddha* means "the Enlightened One." Gautama attained the enlightenment of the Buddha in his final incarnation as Siddhartha Gautama (c. 563–483 B.C.). For forty-five years he preached his doctrine of the Four Noble Truths, the Eightfold Path and the Middle Way, which led to the founding of Buddhism. Gautama Buddha presently holds the office of Lord of the World and is the hierarch of Shamballa, an etheric retreat over the Gobi Desert.

Godfré Ray King. The pen name for Guy W. Ballard, the messenger for the Great White Brotherhood who founded the I AM Movement in the early 1930s under the direction of Saint Germain. He was also embodied as Richard the Lion-Hearted and George Washington. At the end of his life, Mr. Ballard made his ascension and is now known as the Ascended Master Godfre.

Great Central Sun. The Great Central Sun, also called the Great Hub, is the center of cosmos; the point of integration of the Spirit-Matter cosmos and the point of origin of all physical-spiritual creation. The focus of the Great Central Sun in our sector of the galaxy is the God Star, Sirius.

Great White Brotherhood. A spiritual fraternity of ascended masters, archangels and other advanced spiritual beings. The word *white* refers not to race but to the aura (halo) of white light that surrounds these immortals. The Great White Brotherhood works with earnest seekers of every race, religion and walk of life to assist humanity. The Brotherhood also includes certain unascended disciples of the ascended masters.

Heart chakra. Sanskrit name: *Anahata,* meaning "unbeaten" or "unbroken." A twelve-petaled pink chakra located in the center of the chest. It is associated with the third ray and the expression of love, compassion, beauty, selflessness, sensitivity, appreciation, comfort, creativity, charity and generosity.

Higher Self. The I AM Presence and Holy Christ Self; one's innate higher consciousness.

Holy Christ Flame. The threefold flame or divine spark, the flame of God ensconced within the secret chamber of the heart; the soul's point of contact with her I AM Presence and Holy Christ Self.

Holy Christ Self. Our inner teacher, guardian and friend; the advocate and mediator between our soul and God; the universal Christ individualized for each of us.

I AM Presence. The Presence of God, the I AM THAT I AM, individualized for each of us.

I AM THAT I AM. The individualized Presence of God in each soul; the I AM Presence.

Jesus. The Ascended Master Jesus Christ is the avatar of the age of Pisces and an incarnation of the Universal Christ consciousness. He came during his

Galilean embodiment to reveal the individual Christ Self to humanity and to show the works of the Father (the I AM Presence) that can be accomplished by his sons and daughters through the flame of the individual Christ Self. He currently serves with Kuthumi in the office of World Teacher.

John. One of Jesus' chief disciples, the disciple "whom Jesus loved" (John 19:26; 20:2). He made his ascension at the conclusion of that life and is now known as the Ascended Master John the Beloved. John wrote the fourth Gospel, three epistles and the Book of Revelation. His retreat is located in the etheric plane over the Arizona desert.

Karma. (Sanskrit, meaning "act," "deed," "work") Karma, both positive and negative, is the effect of causes we have set in motion in the past, whether ten minutes ago or ten embodiments ago. The law of karma necessitates the soul's reincarnation until all negative karma is balanced.

Karmic Board. A group of eight ascended masters and cosmic beings, also called the Lords of Karma. The ascended masters and lady masters comprising this board are: the Great Divine Director; the Goddess of Liberty; the Ascended Lady Master Nada; the Elohim Cyclopea; Pallas Athena, Goddess of Truth; Portia, Goddess of Justice; and Kuan Yin, Goddess of Mercy. Vairochana, a Buddha of great attainment who has never embodied on earth, became the eighth member of the Karmic Board in 1993. The Lords of Karma dispense justice to this system of worlds, adjudicating karma, mercy and judgment on behalf of every soul. See also Lords of Karma.

Krishna. The eighth and most popular incarnation of Vishnu, the Second Person in the Hindu Trinity of Brahma, Vishnu and Shiva. Krishna focuses God as the Son, the Christ incarnate. Krishna spent his youth (as Gopala) among the cowherds and the gopis (the lovely milkmaids). The gopis were said to be initiates who took incarnation to enjoy the intimate guru-chela relationship with their Lord incarnate. Krishna's childhood (as Govinda) abounds with miracles and playful deeds.

Kuan Yin. The Ascended Lady Master Kuan Yin is known as the Goddess of Mercy because she ensouls the God-qualities of mercy, compassion and forgiveness. Kuan Yin ascended thousands of years ago and has vowed to serve planet Earth until all its evolutions are free. From her etheric retreat, she ministers to the souls of humanity, teaching them to balance their karma and fulfill their divine plan through loving service to life and the application of the violet flame.

Kundalini. (Sanskrit, literally "coiled-up serpent") The sacred fire that lies like a coiled serpent in the base-of-the-spine chakra; also referred to as the light of the Divine Mother. When the kundalini is awakened, it rises through the spinal column to the crown chakra, quickening each of the other chakras on the way.

Kuthumi. The ascended master who serves with Jesus in the office of World Teacher. He is known as the Master Psychologist and is a sponsor of youth. He is also head of the etheric Temple of Illumination in Kashmir and of the Order of the Brothers and Sisters of the Golden Robe. He inspires architects, poets and scientists through divine geometry. His embodiments include Pythagoras, Balthazar (one of the three wise men) and Saint Francis of Assisi. In 1875 he founded the Theosophical Society with El Morya and was known as the Master K.H. or Koot Hoomi.

Lanello. The name of the ascended master who was embodied as Mark L. Prophet, messenger for the Great White Brotherhood. Along with other masters, the Ascended Master Lanello spiritually directs the activities of The Summit Lighthouse from the heaven-world as the "ever-present guru."

Lords of Karma. The ascended masters and cosmic beings who comprise the Karmic Board. The Lords of Karma dispense justice to this system of worlds, adjudicating karma, mercy and judgment on behalf of every soul. All souls must pass before the Karmic Board before and after each incarnation on earth, to receive their assignment and karmic allotment for each lifetime and to review their performance at its conclusion.

Maha Chohan. The hierarch of the seven chohans of the rays. His name means "the Great Lord." He embodies the white light of the seven rays and teaches the balance and integration of these rays. The Maha Chohan is also the representative of the Holy Spirit to earth and her evolutions. Because of his pledge to all mankind to keep the flame until they are able, he is called the Keeper of the Flame.

Mantra. A short spoken prayer consisting of a repeated word or group of words that invokes a particular aspect or quality of God.

Mark L. Prophet. Messenger for the Great White Brotherhood who founded The Summit Lighthouse in 1958 under the direction of the Ascended Master El Morya. At the end of his embodiment in 1973, Mark made his ascension and is now known as the Ascended Master Lanello. After he ascended, his twin flame, the messenger Elizabeth Clare Prophet, carried on the work of The Summit Lighthouse.

Melchizedek. Referred to in the Bible as "king of Salem" and "priest of the most high God" (Gen. 14:18). He is now known as the Ascended Master Melchizedek and he teaches the path of the Melchizedekian priesthood at an etheric retreat over the Caribbean, centered at Cuba.

Mental Body. One of the four lower bodies of man, it consists of the thought processes that make it possible to reason, solve problems and communicate. When quickened, the mental body becomes the vessel for the Christ Self or Christ consciousness.

Messenger. One trained by an ascended master to receive and deliver the teachings, messages and prophecies of the Great White Brotherhood for a people and an age.

Meta. An ascended lady master who serves on the fifth ray (green ray) of healing, science and truth. She is the daughter of Sanat Kumara and Lady Master Venus, hierarchs of the planet Venus. On Atlantis, Meta tended the flame of healing in the healing temple, now focused in the etheric plane over New England. She currently serves in various etheric healing temples and works with all the healing masters and angelic hosts, especially in her ministration to children. She helps parents with their children's problems and heals children's minds from harmful influences. Meta holds the immaculate concept, the pure and perfect crystal design, for every child on earth and those coming into embodiment. Through our calls, we can transfer this crystal matrix to the etheric bodies of our children.

Mother Mary. Mother of Jesus Christ. Her name means Mother Ray (Ma-ray). Throughout her embodiments on earth, she ardently exemplified the Motherhood of God. Mother Mary is now an ascended lady master who is known as a great healer and intercessor on behalf of mankind. She teaches the science of the immaculate concept—the ability to hold the image of the perfect pattern for any part of life and thereby help to bring it into manifestation. She is the twin flame of Archangel Raphael.

Mystery schools. Retreats of the Great White Brotherhood that are specialized repositories of God's knowledge on earth. These retreats establish and uphold the responsible use of divine energy. Past mystery schools include the Garden of Eden, the Sangha of Gautama Buddha, the community of Essenes at Qumran, and Pythagoras' School at Crotona.

Omri-Tas. The Ruler of the Violet Planet, who carries such an intensity of violet flame and the seventh ray in his aura that it extends far beyond the size of planet Earth. The evolutions of the Violet Planet have served the violet flame for aeons, and they use the violet flame to tend to all their daily needs—to clean their homes, to care for and purify the planet, and even to bathe themselves. Menial chores are performed by violet-flame angels and elementals, which allows the people time to pursue the path of adeptship and to serve other planetary homes. Omri-Tas has released specific violet-flame dispensations to assist the students of the ascended masters and to uplift the earth. It is important to call to Omri-Tas to reactivate and multiply these dispensations.

Progressive revelation. The ongoing revelation of spiritual truths to mankind, especially through messages, or dictations. Ascended masters, archangels and other advanced spiritual beings deliver their dictations to mankind through appointed messengers of the Great White Brotherhood.

Reincarnation. The rebirth of a soul in a new human body. The soul continues to return to the physical plane in a new body until she has balanced her karma, attained self-mastery and fulfilled the spiritual requirements for reunion with her I AM Presence in the ritual of the ascension.

Saint Francis of Assisi. (c. 1181–1226) An embodiment of the Ascended Master Kuthumi. Known as the "divine poverello," he renounced his family and wealth to embrace "Lady Poverty." He lived among the poor and the lepers, finding profound joy in imitating the compassion of Christ. In 1209 he founded the Franciscan Order of the Friars Minor.

Saint Germain. Chohan of the Seventh Ray, the violet ray, of freedom and transmutation; Hierarch of the Aquarian Age and sponsor of the United States of America. Saint Germain also initiates souls in the ritual of transmutation through the violet flame by the power of the spoken Word, meditation and visualization.

Saint Teresa of Avila. (1515–1582) A Catholic mystic who was a contemporary and close friend of Saint John of the Cross. In 1970 she was proclaimed the first woman to be made Doctor of the Church, a title given to those who show a high degree of sanctity and eminent learning. In her final embodiment as Florence Jeannette Miller, she assisted the messengers Mark and Elizabeth Prophet. After she made the transition on September 19, 1979, she made her ascension and is now known as the Ascended Lady Master Kristine. Throughout her embodiments she demonstrated the deep love of her heart through sacrifice, surrender, selflessness and service.

Saint Thérèse of Lisieux. (1873–1897) A French Carmelite nun known as the Little Flower of Jesus. She considered it her mission to teach souls her "little way," the way of "spiritual childhood, the way of trust and absolute self-surrender." Saint Thérèse ascended at the end of that embodiment and is now known as the Ascended Lady Master Thérèse of Lisieux.

Science of the Spoken Word. The science of invoking the light of God to produce constructive change in oneself and the world. Practitioners use the science of the spoken Word in affirmations, spoken prayers, and mantras to access divine energy from the Christ Self, the I AM Presence, and the ascended masters and direct it into conditions needing transformation.

Seat-of-the-soul chakra. Sanskrit name: *Svadhishthana,* meaning "sweetness" or "abode of the self." A six-petaled violet chakra located midway between the navel and the base of the spine. It is associated with the seventh ray and the expression of freedom, mercy, forgiveness, justice, transcendence, alchemy, transmutation, diplomacy, intuition, prophecy and revelation.

Secret chamber of the heart. A spiritual chamber behind and to the left of the heart chakra, which is surrounded by great light and protection. It is the connecting point of the cord of light that descends from each one's I AM Presence to sustain the beating of the physical heart, giving life, purpose and cosmic integration. It is the special place where one communes with the Holy Christ Self and fans the fires of the threefold flame.

Secret-ray chakras. The five minor chakras that correspond to the five secret rays. They are located in the hands, the feet and the chest, the same places where Jesus Christ was nailed to the cross and his body was pierced.

Serapis Bey. Chohan of the Fourth Ray, the white ray, of purity; the ascended master who prepares and trains candidates for the ascension. Serapis Bey is the hierarch of the Ascension Temple, a retreat located in the etheric plane at Luxor, Egypt.

Seven Rays. The seven spiritual light rays of God; the seven rays that emerge out of the white light of the Christ consciousness. Each ray focuses a frequency, or color, and has specific qualities. First ray: blue—faith, will, power, perfection and protection; Second ray: yellow—wisdom, understanding, enlightenment and illumination; Third ray: pink—compassion, kindness, charity, love and beauty; Fourth ray: white—purity, discipline, order and joy; Fifth ray: green—truth, science, healing, music, abundance and vision; Sixth ray: purple and gold with flecks of ruby—ministration, service, peace and brotherhood; Seventh ray: violet—freedom, mercy, justice, transmutation and forgiveness.

Solar-plexus chakra. Sanskrit name: *Manipura,* meaning "city of jewels" or "filled with jewels." A ten-petaled chakra located at the navel, its colors are purple and gold with ruby flecks. It is associated with the sixth ray and the expression of peace, brotherhood, selfless service, right desire, balance and harmlessness.

Soul. The soul is the living potential of God, projected from the I AM Presence into physical evolution. The soul is not immortal but can attain immortality through fusion with the Holy Christ Self and the I AM Presence in the ritual of the ascension. Since the soul is the feminine counterpart of the Spirit (the masculine polarity) we refer to the soul as "she," regardless of whether it is the soul of a man or a woman.

Spirit. The masculine polarity of the Godhead, in relationship to the feminine coordinate of matter. God as Father, of necessity, includes within the polarity of himself God as Mother and is therefore known as the Father-Mother God. The plane of the I AM Presence; the dwelling place of the ascended masters in the kingdom of God.

Summit University. A modern-day mystery school founded in 1971 under the direction of the messengers, Mark L. Prophet and Elizabeth Clare Prophet. At Summit University, students study the teachings of the ascended masters delivered through their messengers.

The Summit Lighthouse. An outer organization of the Great White Brotherhood. Mark L. Prophet founded The Summit Lighthouse in 1958 under the direction of the Ascended Master El Morya to publish the teachings of the ascended masters.

Third-eye chakra. Sanskrit name: *Ajna,* meaning "to command." An emerald green chakra located between the eyebrows. It is associated with the fifth ray and the expression of truth, divine vision, holding the highest vision for oneself and others, healing, wholeness, abundance, clarity, constancy, focus, music and science.

Threefold flame. The divine spark, the flame of God ensconced within the secret chamber of the heart as three plumes of love, wisdom and power; the soul's point of contact with her I AM Presence and Holy Christ Self.

Throat chakra. Sanskrit name: *Vishuddha,* meaning "pure" or "purity." A sixteen-petaled blue chakra located at the throat. It is associated with the first ray and the expression of power, will, faith, protection, direction, courage and obedience.

Tube of light. The white light that descends from the heart of the I AM Presence in answer to the individual's call. About nine feet in diameter, it is a cylinder that originates in the I AM Presence and extends three feet below the person's feet. The tube of light acts as a shield of protection from negative energies and is sustained for twenty-four hours as long as one invokes it daily and maintains harmony in his thoughts, feelings, words and deeds.

Twin flame. Every soul has her divine counterpart or twin flame. Each set of twin flames is created out of a white-fire body in the heart of the Great Central Sun. The white-fire body divides into two identical spheres, each consisting of an I AM Presence surrounded by a causal body. The I AM Presence of each one then sends forth the soul of a twin flame. For the purposes of the incarnation and evolution of twin flames, the two souls are in polarity to each other, one representing the masculine and the other the feminine half of the Divine Whole. These polarities may alternate in succeeding incarnations. Twin flames share a unique electronic blueprint and a unique cosmic destiny. They reunite permanently when both souls have made their ascension.

Violet flame. The seventh ray aspect of the Holy Spirit. The sacred fire that transmutes the cause, effect, record, and memory of sin, or negative karma. Also called the flame of transmutation, of freedom and of forgiveness. When the violet flame is invoked through the science of the spoken Word, it brings about powerful, constructive change.

Web of light. A synonym for antahkarana, the web of life, or network of light spanning Spirit and matter. The web of light connects and sensitizes all within it to one another and to the heart of God.

Zarathustra. The Ascended Master Zarathustra was embodied as the prophet who founded the Zoroastrian religion among the Parsees in Persia, the area now known as Iran. In about 600 B.C. at the age of 30, he received a series of visions from Ahura Mazda, the "Wise Lord" or "Lord who bestows intelligence" (the Ancient of Days, known in the East as Sanat Kumara and Karttikeya). Ahura Mazda revealed his name when Zarathustra said: "Tell me, O Pure Ahura Mazda, the name which is Thy greatest, best, fairest, and which is the most efficacious for prayer." Ahura Mazda answered: "My first name is I AM . . . and my twentieth name is I AM THAT I AM, Mazda."

FURTHER STUDY

Books by Summit University Press

These books can be ordered from The Summit Lighthouse, 63 Summit Way, Gardiner, MT 59030.
To place an order or request a catalog:
Go to www.SummitLighthouse.org • E-mail TSLinfo@TSL.org
Call 1-800-245-5445 or 406-848-9500 • Fax 1-800-221-8307 or 406-848-9555

ACCESS THE POWER OF YOUR HIGHER SELF
by Elizabeth Clare Prophet
Your Higher Self is your Real Self. The self that you identify with today is just a tiny fraction of the mighty being that you are. Learn how to connect with the Higher Self, how to access its unlimited energy, and how to protect and sustain this contact throughout the day.
POCKET GUIDE 110 PP. # 4423

ANGELS
(decree booklet)
by Elizabeth Clare Prophet
Words to decrees, mantras, songs and bhajans celebrating the seven archangels and the seven rays. The pages are color coded according to the seven rays.
BOOKLET 18 PP. #3600

THE ANSWER YOU'RE LOOKING FOR IS INSIDE OF YOU
A Commonsense Guide to Spiritual Growth
by Mark L. Prophet
Weaves anecdotes from everyday life with universal truths to create a profound yet thoroughly enjoyable guide to spiritual growth. Mark Prophet, one of the great spiritual teachers of our time, believed that our quest for meaning in life, though challenging, should be fun.
SOFTBOUND 118 PP. #4378

THE CHELA AND THE PATH
Keys to Soul Mastery in the Aquarian Age
by El Morya
Contains personal instruction from El Morya for all spiritual seekers and chelas (students of a spiritual teacher). It is foundational for those who would not only know their true potential, but fulfill it.
SOFTBOUND 164 PP. #420

THE CREATIVE POWER OF SOUND
Affirmations to Create, Heal and Transform
by Elizabeth Clare Prophet
For centuries, mystics of East and West have believed that sound creates matter. Seven fundamental principles for using prayers, affirmations, decrees and mantras to generate spiritual energy.
POCKET GUIDE 108 PP. #4447

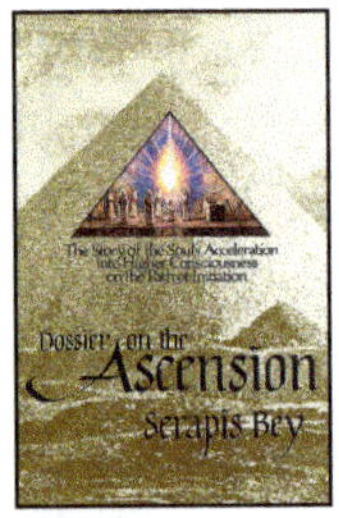

DOSSIER ON THE ASCENSION
The Story of the Soul's Acceleration into Higher Consciousness on the Path of Initiation
by Serapis Bey
A profound look into the life of the soul, her purpose and destiny. Practical keys for spiritual growth that can lead to the attainment of the ascension.
SOFTBOUND 216 PP. #1038

HEART, HEAD AND HAND DECREES
A convenient pocket-size booklet of meditations, affirmations, mantras, prayers and decrees for contacting and increasing the divine qualities of power, wisdom and love within you.
BOOKLET 48 PP. #4444

THE HUMAN AURA
How to Activate and Energize Your Aura and Chakras
by Kuthumi and Djwal Kul
In this book, Kuthumi unveils the mysteries of the human aura, from the meaning of its colors to how you can strengthen, purify, expand and protect it. Djwal Kul reveals the science of the chakras and their relationship to the aura.
POCKETBOOK 442 PP. #1483

KEEPERS OF THE FLAME FRATERNITY BROCHURE
Gives information on and includes an enrollment form for the Keepers of the Flame Fraternity, an inner society of the ascended masters. As a member of this nondenominational fraternity, you will receive thirty-three monthly lessons and personal sponsorship from the Ascended Master Saint Germain.
FREE BROCHURE

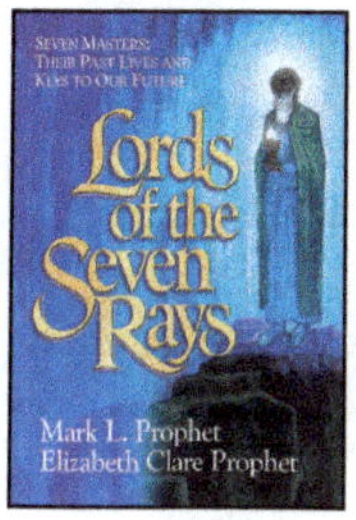

LORDS OF THE SEVEN RAYS
Seven Masters: Their Past Lives and Keys to Our Future
by Mark L. Prophet and Elizabeth Clare Prophet
Tells the stories of seven mystics who reached for and accomplished the goal of self-transcendence on each of the seven initiatic paths or "rays" of spiritual growth.
SOFTBOUND 428 PP. #2079

THE PATH TO YOUR ASCENSION
Rediscovering Life's Ultimate Purpose
by Annice Booth
This book will help you rediscover what your soul has known from the beginning—that life does have a higher purpose. It shapes the wisdom of the ascended masters into a personal guide for your own soul's liberation.
SOFTBOUND 270 PP. #4457

PRAYERS, MEDITATIONS AND DYNAMIC DECREES
for Personal and World Transformation
Your complete handbook of decrees for personal and world action. 500 color-coded loose-leaf pages, 3-hole punched.
#1778

REINCARNATION
The Missing Link in Christianity
by Elizabeth Clare Prophet with Erin L. Prophet
A provocative work that makes the case that Jesus taught reincarnation. Using evidence from the Dead Sea Scrolls and Gnostic texts, the authors argue persuasively that Jesus was a mystic who taught that our destiny is to unite with the God within.
SOFTBOUND 430 PP. #4380

THE SCIENCE OF THE SPOKEN WORD
by Mark L. Prophet and Elizabeth Clare Prophet
The authors present the most powerful and profound message on techniques of spoken prayer in print today. This important work explains how to use worded formulas to access the full spectrum of spiritual light for personal and world transformation.
SOFTBOUND 246 PP. #104

SOUL MATES AND TWIN FLAMES
The Spiritual Dimension of Love and Relationships
by Elizabeth Clare Prophet
"Extremely powerful in revealing the inner mysteries of the soul and the true essence of love through its insightful analysis of real-life experiences and classical love stories." —Marilyn Barrick, Ph.D., author of *Emotions: Transforming Anger, Fear and Pain.*
POCKET GUIDE 166 PP. #4465

VIOLET FLAME TO HEAL BODY, MIND AND SOUL
by Elizabeth Clare Prophet
Describes how to use violet flame—a unique high-frequency spiritual energy—to increase vitality and spirituality, overcome blocks to healing and transmute the burden of traumatic experiences.
POCKET GUIDE 108 PP. #4424

I AM YOUR GUARD
How Archangel Michael Can Protect You
by Elizabeth Clare Prophet
Terrorism. War. Earth changes. Violent crime. The threats to our families, nations and environment are enormous. Now more than ever, we need Archangel Michael. This breakthrough book will introduce you to Archangel Michael and how you can call for his protection. Revered in Jewish, Christian and Islamic traditions, Archangel Michael can protect you and your loved ones in times of trouble. All you need to know is how to ask for his help. This book shows you how.
POCKET GUIDE 112 PP. #7268

Gardens of the Heart

Each book in the series is a collection of meaningful quotes that can lift the spirit, unfold understanding and gently guide the reader to the garden within his or her own heart.

COMPASSION
Gardens of the Heart

Compassion can be an instrument for profound healing—bringing one to a new sense of wholeness and understanding. We all make mistakes. Compassion recognizes suffering and moves heaven and earth to alleviate it. SOFTBOUND #6002 130 PP.

FORGIVENESS
Gardens of the Heart

Forgiveness has the power to transform one's life and heal wounds of the heart and mind. As we forgive ourselves, we will be able to forgive others. As we forgive others, we will be forgiven… SOFTBOUND #6001 130 PP.

JOY
Gardens of the Heart

Joy comes from an appreciation of things small and great, of life in the moment—a glistening dewdrop, the face of a child, a smile. SOFTBOUND #6004 130 PP.

GRATITUDE
Gardens of the Heart

In gratitude, give of yourself. See how you become more refined, more of your greater self. SOFTBOUND #6003 130 PP.

Other Books

AUTOBIOGRAPHY OF A YOGI
by Paramahansa Yogananda
(Los Angeles: Self-Realization Fellowship, 1977)

THE CHAKRAS *by C. W. Leadbeater*
rev. ed. (Wheaton, Ill.: The Theosophical Publishing House, 1994)

A DWELLER ON TWO PLANETS *by Phylos the Thibetan* (Vista, Calif.: Borden Publishing Co., 1952)

HOW TO KNOW GOD
trans. by Swami Prabhavananda and Christopher Isherwood (Hollywood, Calif.: Vedanta Press, 1987)

KARMA-YOGA AND BHAKTI-YOGA
by Swami Vivekananda
(New York: Ramakrishna-Vivekananda Center, 1982)

LIFE AFTER LIFE *by Raymond A. Moody, Jr.*
(New York: Bantam Books, 1976)

LIFE BEFORE LIFE *by Helen Wambach*
(New York: Bantam Books, 1979)

LIFE BETWEEN LIFE
by Joel L. Whitton and Joe Fisher
(New York: Warner Books, 1986)

REINCARNATION ***The Phoenix Fire Mystery***
compiled and edited by Joseph Head and S. L. Cranston (New York: Julian Press, 1977)

SAVED BY THE LIGHT
by Dannion Brinkley with Paul Perry
(New York: Random House, Inc., 1994)

UNVEILED MYSTERIES *by Godfré Ray King*
(Chicago: Saint Germain Press, 1982)

ONLINE COURSES

With Summit University online courses, you can study spiritual teachings in the comfort of your own home, or anywhere you have access to the Internet. Each course provides you with readings, spiritual and journaling exercises, audio and video clips, online forum discussions, recommendations for further study, and an instructor who will answer your questions. Visit www.SummitUniversity.org and keep checking back for new courses.

THE VICTORY WAY OF LIFE
How to Conquer Adversity and Thrive!
Work with Mighty Victory to develop a positive attitude, overcome self-defeating habits, and join forces with Victory's angels to solve challenging issues in society.
RELS 0201

RELATIONSHIPS: EXPLORE THE MYSTERIES OF SOUL MATES AND TWIN FLAMES
Keys to Successful Relationships.
This course helps men and women of all ages explore the spiritual dimension of relationships and find new keys to wholeness and true love. **RELS 0301**

UNVEILED MYSTERIES
Unite with God's Light and Be Free!
In this course, Elizabeth Clare Prophet goes deeply into the mysteries of the book *Unveiled Mysteries* by Godfré Ray King, and teaches on what it takes to have a face-to-face encounter with an ascended master and your own Higher Self.
RELS 0701

THE EMERALD MATRIX: A FORMULA FOR TRUE INNER HEALING
Activate Your Inner Healer.
Learn how to create a unique personal healing formula, or Emerald Matrix, that will help you heal yourself in body, mind and soul. **META 0501**

THE MAGIC POWER OF COSMIC LAW
Discover the Why in Everything.
Cosmic laws are affecting you whether you realize it or not. The more you know about them, the more you will be able to answer the question "Why are things in life the way they are?" and harness these cosmic laws to create positive change in your world.
META 0401

ASCENSION: THE GOAL OF LIFE
Reunite with God in the Ritual of the Ascension!
Based on the book *Dossier on the Ascension* by Serapis Bey, Elizabeth Clare Prophet delivers inspiring commentary on the path to your ascension and tells the compelling story of your soul's acceleration into higher consciousness. Contains profound keys to the mystery of your ascension! **META 0410**

WHAT IS THE ASCENSION? (Mini Course) ***Life Has a Higher Purpose!***
What is the ascension? What are the necessary requirements for your soul's acceleration on the spiritual path? Learn practical techniques for spiritual growth and transform your life. **ME 01**

WHEN THE MASTERS SPEAK: HOW TO STUDY DICTATIONS
(Mini Course) Learn how to study dictations by the ascended masters so you can apply their profound instructions to your daily life. **ME 02**

HOME STUDY COURSES

For those who prefer reading as opposed to studying online, Summit University offers several self-guided study materials. These step-by-step guides bring you closer to your higher self and the ascended masters and provide practical tools for personal spiritual growth.

SACRED ADVENTURE 1
The Spiritual Quest
by the Staff of Summit University
This comprehensive introduction to the Teachings of the Ascended Masters® gives you the keys to get in touch with your soul's inner power. It includes seven interactive lessons with profound teachings, true stories, illustrations, exercises, meditations and accelerated spiritual techniques to help transform yourself and your world.

SACRED ADVENTURE 2
Meeting the Masters
by the Staff of Summit University
The second book in the Sacred Adventure series introduces you to the seven spiritual rays and the ascended masters who instruct us in their use. You'll come face-to-face with the masters of the first three rays: El Morya, Lord Lanto and Paul the Venetian. Come to know them intimately as you learn about their lives and passions. In addition to transformative spiritual exercises, this book also contains exciting chapters on soul travel, hierarchy, working with angels and expanding the divine spark in your heart.

SACRED ADVENTURE 3
Working with the Masters
by the Staff of Summit University
The third book in the Sacred Adventure series completes the overview of the seven rays. You'll be introduced to the ascended masters Serapis Bey, Hilarion, Nada and Saint Germain and will learn about the Divine Mother, the creative power of music and the mysterious world of the elemental builders of form. The book concludes with instructions on how to pursue your own path of personal Christhood as a student of one of the Lords of the Seven Rays.

WALKING WITH THE MASTER
Answering the Call of Jesus
by Elizabeth Clare Prophet and Staff of Summit University
Two thousand years ago Jesus called a small group of disciples to leave their nets and follow him. He gave them a teaching and a path of initiation, only fragments of which are found in the New Testament. This path is as real and as vital today as it was in Jesus' time. And now, at the turning of an age, the ascended master Jesus calls those who would be his disciples to take up that path to walk and work with him again. Twenty-eight steps on that path are presented here, with commentary and explanation by Elizabeth Clare Prophet and the staff of Summit University. The goal is to find and externalize the Christ within. The means is a practical path of initiation for the modern world.

SEMINARS

Every year, Summit University hosts many seminars in locations throughout the world. These powerful, affordable weekend events on a variety of spiritual topics including healing, psychology, and spiritual development, give you the opportunity to spend quality time with yourself and with God, and explore the next step on your spiritual path.

www.SummitUniversity.org

Mark L. Prophet (1918–1973) and Elizabeth Clare Prophet (1939–2009), were visionary pioneers of modern spirituality and internationally renowned authors. Their books are published in more than 30 languages, and millions of copies have been sold online and in bookstores worldwide.

Together, they built a worldwide spiritual organization that is helping thousands to find their way out of human problems and reconnect to their inner divinity. They walked the path of spiritual adeptship, advancing through the universal initiations common to mystics of both East and West. They taught about this path and described their own experiences for the benefit of all who desire to make spiritual progress.

Mark and Elizabeth left an extensive library of spiritual teachings from the ascended masters and a thriving, worldwide community of people who study and practice these teachings.

Summit University®
63 Summit Way
Gardiner, Montana 59030 USA

1-800-245-5445 / 406-848-9500

Se habla español.

SummitUniversity.org

TSLinfo@TSL.org

SummitLighthouse.org

SacredAdventureSeries.org

CPSIA information can be obtained
at www.ICGtesting.com
Printed in the USA
FSHW020005070821

9 781609 882983